2.25

OFFICIAL'S MANUAL:
SOCCER

6916

DEDICATION

To Jean, Missy, Leslie, Cricket and Matthew.

ACKNOWLEDGEMENTS

For their support, input, cooperation and overall dedication to the advancement of the game of soccer, the improvement of soccer officiating and the completion of this book, expressions of gratitude are extended to Rue Davidson, Don Dennison, Jim Devaney, Tarek Khan, Dick Lafferty, Alan Lowe, Bob Rogers, Joe Short, Bob Sommers, Paul Suchoski, Dirk Van Der Loo and Diana Weaver. Special thanks also go to University of Maryland Head Soccer Coach Jim Dietsch, members of his 1978 varsity and the former Maryland players who took the time from their annual Alumni-Varsity game to pose for pictures.

N.K.

OFFICIAL'S MANUAL:
SOCCER

Toward Better Soccer Officiating

Nick Kovalakides

Leisure Press
P.O. Box 3
West Point, N.Y. 10996

A publication of Leisure Press.
P.O. Box 3, West Point, N.Y. 10996
Copyright © 1978 by Nick Kovalakides
All rights reserved. Printed in the U.S.A.

ISBN 0-918438-50-0

All photos by Pete Dykstra

4

Table of Contents

List of Illustrations

Preface

The sport of soccer has reached the stage in most parts of the United States wherein the soccer coach no longer has to wait and see who gets cut from the football team in order to determine the candidates for his soccer team. In some areas, being part of the soccer team is just as prestigious as being a member of the football team. In other areas, it is even *more* prestigious.

Local fan support has also frequently been split between the two "major" fall sports. With that in mind, athletic directors schedule the two sports at different times so that they will not compete with each other for community backing.

Students are now entering high school with anywhere from one to eight years of competitive playing experience under their belts. Credit for this goes to the thousands of youth clubs which are jammed with more and more youngsters each year seeking a chance to play the game.

Parents are recognizing that soccer is not as expensive as football with regard to personal equipment. In other comparisons with football, they see soccer as a game with just as much a need for teamwork and individual effort and commitment, but with less chance for serious injury. While the football player may never do anything but block in the line, each soccer player gets to play the ball. Soccer also gives the players more continuous exercise over relatively the same time period.

With all of this experience, players and spectators have become more aware of the rules of the game and the intricacies surrounding game strategy. By the same token, no longer can an official expect to call a game without being challenged if he demonstrates limited ability to keep a game under control or minimal knowledge of the rules.

Soccer officials must always seek to improve their efficiency and performance. Officials associations are becoming more professional in requiring examinations of their rookie referees and retesting of their veteran members.

Preface

The officials are constantly being evaluated by their peers and by the coaches. Clinics on rule interpretations and mechanics are conducted regularly throughout the season.

This book is designed primarily to help those officials who are assigned mostly to games which use the dual-referee system and the rules of the National Collegiate Athletic Association and the National Federation of State High School Associations. This does not mean that none of the material would apply to officials working games themselves with the aid of two linespersons under Federation of International Football Association rules. To the contrary, with the possible exception of items pertaining to partner coordination, the entire book is applicable to all soccer referees officiating at all levels.

It is hoped that each reader will find something which will help him toward being a better soccer official.

Nick Kovalakides

CHAPTER I

Your Philosophy and Professional Attitude

"If something is worth doing, it is worth doing it well." This should be part of your personal creed as a soccer referee. You should always strive to improve your officiating. You should watch the best referees in your association when they work a game. Learn by imitation. Listen, watch and learn from each of your game partners. Benefit by recognizing the mistakes of others and avoid making the same ones yourself.

In order to be a top-notch referee, you must enjoy officiating. You must take pride in knowing that your game is kept under control and played according to the rules and that each team has a fair chance to win. You must always remain cognizant of the three teams on the field—the home team, the visiting team and the *team* of officials.

It should bother you to make a mistake, use poor judgment or miss a call because you were out of position. On the other hand, it should make you feel good that, when a similar occasion arises, you do not make the same mistake twice. You should also take pride in making a difficult or unusual call in the crucial part of the game when your call exemplifies hours of studying the rules and self-confidence in the manner in which you enforced those rules.

When you approach EACH of your games with enthusiasm, honesty, sincerity and consistency, everyone at the game—the players, the coaches and the spectators—will appreciate it and you will feel it through their sincerest compliment—their silence toward you. Ultimately, however, you will feel best when you are satisfied that yours was a job well done.

Knowing the Rules

As an official, you must know the rules of the game and how to correctly and effectively enforce them. Knowing the rules is paramount, but without the proper enforcement methods, officiating success comes slowly. Correctly enforcing the rules is important, but in doing so, you must be effective. That means that the players, coaches, spectators and your partner must recognize early that your calls are being made for the betterment of the game.

There is no excuse for an official misapplying a rule or making up one of his own rules. It is important that you have several copies of the rulebook close at hand and in various places so that you can easily get to one whenever you find yourself with time on your hands. Have one in your car in case you run into a traffic jam and have to stop; or when you are waiting for someone who is late. Perhaps one would be useful on your bed stand or in your bathroom! Whenever you get the chance, read and *study a different rule each time.*

It is imperative that each word of a rule is read carefully and its meaning understood. As an example, what would be your call in this situation: You have called tripping against Team A in the middle of the field and about five yards outside Team B's penalty area. You have awarded a direct free kick to Team B. Noticing that the Team A players have moved upfield, the Team B kicker turns around quickly and kicks the ball back toward his goalkeeper so that he would be able to punt it further upfield.

His quickness, however, catches his own goalkeeper off guard and the ball goes directly into his own goal. Goal for Team A? Or corner kick for Team A?

If it had not been a free kick situation, it would have been a goal for Team A. However, the correct call is a corner kick for Team A, because the definition of Direct Free Kick is "one on which a goal can be scored directly from the kick *against the offending team".* That means that it cannot be scored directly from the kick against the *offended* team.

Accepting Game Assignments

Never accept a game assignment when you can be associated in any manner with either team. If you know any of the players personally, or are related to any of them or if one of the teams is from your alma mater or school district, you should notify your commissioner accordingly to get your assignment changed. These relationships would affect you subconsciously and since there is enough pressure on you already to call a fair game, these situations should be avoided entirely. This is not to imply that you would purposely slight one team or the other; however, no matter how hard you would try to make calls as you see them, if Team A finds out that you are related in some way to Team B, there will be overtones automatically applied to any call that you make that goes against Team A.

If you are assigned to a school or field for the first time, get the directions well in advance. Do not wait until leaving for the game to check the map. Leave ample time in case you get lost and/or run into heavy traffic.

You should arrive with ample time to (1) check the field and its markings, goals, nets and corner flags as well as the players' equipment, (2) confer with your partner on mechanics, (3) greet the coaches and verify the local rules, (4) do some stretching and warm-up exercises, and (5) conduct the pre-game ceremony with the captains, so that the game will start on time. Teams should never have to wait for an official, although you would be expected to wait patiently for a team if it were late in arriving.

Making A Good Impression

When appearing on the field, you should be completely dressed—no last-minute stuffing your shirttail in, pulling your socks up or tying your shoe-laces. Remember how lasting first impressions are.

Act as a professional at all times. Never voluntarily fraternize with players, coaches, parents or spectators. This type of conduct is almost invariably interpreted as showing favoritism to one team. If these people approach you in a fraternizing manner, simply greet them cheerfully, exchange small talk, but only briefly and then excuse yourself gracefully indicating that you must go about your business of getting the game started on time.

Never, absolutely never, get a ball and begin to kick it around or bounce it several times off your foot, knee, or whatever, in attempt to show off your soccer skills. In doing so, you are virtually asking the players, coaches and spectators to look upon you as a player rather than as an official.

Personal Appearance and Equipment

Your personal appearance should be neat and clean. Your uniform should be neat and clean. You should be well-groomed. If you show up with a dirty uniform and/or muddy shoes, people will get the impression that you do not believe that their game is very important or that you are a leftover from another game. While it may be true, you should never admit that you have just awakened, had a bad day at work, or are worried that officiating this game will make you late for another engagement. Everyone should get the feeling that the only thing that you have had planned for your day is to officiate their game.

Wear the prescribed uniform (Fig. 1), but make sure that yours matches your partner's. If the pants are to be black, that does not mean gray or dark blue. Faded uniforms should be replaced by new ones. Furthermore, avoid colorful undergarments which will show through your uniform as they will

11

Figure 1. Prescribed Uniforms. No matter which uniform is required by your chapter, association or league, be certain that yours matches your partner's.

Figure 2. Recommended Wrist Stopwatch and Finger Whistle. Both allow for handling the ball with ease.

detract from your overall appearance. Stick with white or black under-garments.

In many areas, games below the college level require the referee to keep the time on the field; therefore, it would be wise to invest in a *wrist* stop-watch as opposed to one which you must hold in your hand. (Fig. 2) Having the watch on your wrist not only frees your hands to handle the ball or anything else, but it can also be read easily at almost any time. Furthermore, if you want to make sure that you have pushed the button hard enough to start it running, you merely need to raise your wrist to your ear and listen to it without having to take your eyes off of the game.

Make sure, of course, that your stopwatch has two buttons — one to start and stop it and the other to return both hands to zero. Watches to be avoid-ed are those with only one button, because pushing it once starts it, pushing it again stops it, but pushing it a third time sends it back to zero. This type of watch is useless since you will have to stop and restart it several times for goals, injuries, penalty kicks, etc.

While a wrist stopwatch is recommended, a finger whistle is also prefer-able. This type of whistle sits on top of two finger rings. (Fig. 2) It looks like part of a set of brass knuckles. They are very popular with football referees. Once again, your hand is free to handle the ball, etc. More importantly, however, it forces you into the habit of carrying the whistle in your hand in-stead of in your mouth.

Many new officials like to have their whistle in their mouths so that they will be able to blow it quickly, perhaps to impress the coaches with their fast reflexes. This may be a valid thought; however, there will come the time when you see an infraction, instinctively blow your whistle and then realize that you have penalized the wrong team when, in actuality, a "play on" situation had existed. An official who blows his whistle inadvertently is usually the one who carries it in his mouth. Having the whistle in your hand enables you to use the time that it takes to raise it to your mouth to see if you should call "play on" instead. A good motto to follow: "It is better to be late and correct, than it is to be quick and wrong."

With regard to personal equipment, it is most important to have your watch and whistle in good working condition. Nevertheless, it is simply basic to make sure that you have *all* of your equipment with you when you walk onto the playing field. There is nothing more embarrassing or unprofessional than for an official to ask a coach for a spare whistle or for a coin to flip.

Remember, in school, how you would make sets of initials in order to memorize a list of things for a science quiz or a history test? Here is a way to remember all of your personal equipment: WWCCPP. **W**atch and **W**histles (two are recommended), **C**ards (red and yellow) and **C**oin, **P**encil and **P**aper. (Fig. 3) Some yellow cards are made with a textured material which makes it

13

Figure 3. Personal Equipment—"WWCCPP". Watch and Whistles (two are recommended), Cards (red and yellow) and Coin, Pencil and Paper.

easy to write on them with a pencil. These could serve to replace the pad of paper.

When driving your car directly to the field and already in uniform, the problem of where to put your keys becomes a concern. If you have a large number of keys, it is wise to detach only your car door key, while leaving the others in the car, perhaps under the seat or floor mat. If you have no pockets, you could run your shoelace through the hole in the key and carry it tied to your shoe. Naturally, it would be imperative not to have frayed shoelaces.

CHAPTER II

Before The Game

When arriving at the school or field, be sure to park in an area so that you will not be delayed in leaving after the game. Avoid parking near the visiting team bus or where many of the home players and spectators will be walking after the game. It is not that you should expect the players and coaches to be belligerent toward you, it is merely considered good preventive officiating in not being around these areas or people in case the game does not go well for them and they would want to vent their frustrations on you. You must realize that after each game 50% of the people are happy and the other half are not. It is an accepted fact that many teams and their followers will blame their loss on the officials. Consequently, there is no sense in giving them the opportunity to show you how they feel. Plan ahead for a swift and smooth exit.

For the same reasons, you should arrive dressed in your uniform, so as to avoid having to dress in the coach's office. However, if you must, it would be wise to dress there before the game only and then take your clothes and lock them in your car. You would then merely need to leave the area immediately after the game in your referee's uniform only to shower and dress at home or anywhere else, such as an athletic club, on your way back to the office or any other engagement on your day's schedule.

If you have no other choice but to dress in the coach's office after the game, be sure to act as if you are his guest, because, in essence, *you are*. Be sure to have your own towel and soap to avoid borrowing them from him. If he happens to be the losing coach and you can feel him grumbling about it, you should say very little, if anything. Shower, dress and leave as quickly as possible. Now there is no need to rush, but there are problems to be found the longer you hang around. Do not misunderstand the point being made here. You should not expect to be berated or chastised in any way, but be realistic and do not put yourself into a compromising position. However, if a coach does conduct himself toward you in a derogatory manner, you should report them to his principal and to your commissioner.

It is recommended that you arrange to meet your partner on your way to the field or in the field's parking lot, so that both of you may walk onto the field together and inspect the field and greet the coaches together. In this manner, you will look like a team — dignified and authoritative.

Once you appear on the field, your job begins. You should also be aware that all of the players, coaches and spectators will be looking at you and sizing you up. This is when you must make that good first impression. Many veteran coaches take this time to evaluate how professional each referee acts. The coach will watch to see what you do and what you do not do.

One of the first of your pre-game duties should be to jog around the entire field to check the corner flags, goals, nets, field markings and wet or muddy areas. This will show the coaches that you are genuinely concerned that the field meets the standards you expect and it will also show that you know the importance of warming up. Naturally, your jog should be supplemented with some flexibility and stretching exercises. (Fig. 4)

If, while checking the field, you discover some shortcomings such as no center circle, no corner flags, no arc adjacent to the penalty area, etc., you should alert both coaches accordingly. Indicate to them that if these deficiencies cannot be corrected before the game, then you and your partner will simply use your judgement in making calls in these areas. You should also urge the host to remedy these problems before his next home game.

If the line between the goal posts has been obliterated by use, it would be worthwhile to etch a line with the heel of your shoe to assist you in making judgments on shots-on-goal. If necessary, this should be repeated just before a penalty shot.

If rubber highway cones are being used as corner markers, be sure that no part of the conical shape is in the field of play. Similarly, if cones are used on the touch lines to indicate the half-way line, then these cones should be at least one yard outside the touch line. If these cones are permitted to rest on the touch lines, it is conceivable that a ball going out-of-bounds could be prevented from doing so by a marker which is actually unofficial.

Once you have checked the field, you should introduce yourself to each coach. Be certain to greet each with a smile and say "Hi, Coach, I'm John Jones". (Fig. 5) Hopefully, he will return with a similar friendly greeting and give you his name. If he does not give you his name, then simply ask him for it by saying "And you are...?" Make certain, however, that you always address him as "Coach" or "Mr. Smith". In return, you should expect to be call-

Figure 4. Flexibility and Stretching Exercises. Two examples—there are others.

Figure 5. Friendly Greeting for the Coaches.

ed "Ref" or "Mr. Referee". Many coaches look upon officials as villains the moment they step onto the field. This friendly greeting should dissuade him from having such an opinion of you.

Verify the Rules BEFORE The Game

Be sure to get both coaches together with you and your partner to discuss the rules by which the game will be played. (Fig. 6) NCAA rules? FIFA rules? Any local or league rules which are different? How many minutes per half? How will tied games be determined—overtime periods, penalty kicks or left as a tie? Will the overtime periods be sudden death or not? Should the coin be flipped again or will the teams merely switch ends with the team which kicked off at the beginning of the game kicking off again? How and when will substitutions be made?

Once this has been done, do not linger with the coaches in idle conversation, because it will not take long for one of them to describe to you how they think the game will be played. They will say things such as, "Boy, we really need to win this game in order to make it to the playoffs", or "They're a lot stronger than we are, we won't have a chance." All of this, of course, is designed to sway your thinking. There is also the coach who will attempt to get you aside and interrogate you on how well his opponents have played in previous games which you may have officiated. Your only recourse is to avoid giving any kind of specific answer.

Figure 6. Verifying the Rules BEFORE the Game.

Your Thoughts on the Game

Your thinking on the game should be non-existent. To you, this game should be between the "blue shirts" and the "red shirts" and it is for the championship. You should not be concerned in any manner with who the teams are, what their win-loss records are, nor who the best players are. You should never ask a coach how his team has been doing. You should avoid reading about these teams in the newspaper. You should have an open mind. Your only thoughts should be to insure that both teams will have an equal chance to win the game according to the rules and that the game will remain under control.

If you know anything special about either team or any of the players, it will subconsciously affect you when making a call. You may find yourself thinking that an undefeated team would not be guilty of tripping, or you might overlook that extended elbow when it belongs to the player who has made the all-star list for the past two years, or you might choose not to give a yellow card to a 15-year veteran coach when he adamantly dissents with one of your calls. On the other hand, knowing some of these things about the players and the teams just might make you lean the other way wherein you would be picayune or extra harsh on them.

Paying Attention to Details

While the teams are completing their warmups, look around for players wearing jewelry, casts and any other items which may become dangerous during play. Take care of these problems then, so that you will not have to stop play during the game to do something that you should have taken care of before the game.

Satisfy yourself that the teams' shirt colors are enough of a contrast that it will not cause you any problems in deciphering the players when they are in front of the goal going for the ball and having a great deal of body contact. For the same reasons, plus the fact that the goalkeeper is allowed to handle the ball in the penalty area, you should make certain that each goalkeeper's shirt color differs from all other players including the opposing goalkeeper. Once again, take care of this *before the game* and not after you have called a player for handling the ball in the penalty area only to discover that he is the goalkeeper wearing a shirt similar to that of his teammates.

Do not be talked into allowing a goalkeeper to wear a shirt which is only slightly different from either team. After all, you are the one who will have to make the calls. It would help if the goalkeeper wore a long-sleeved shirt, so that when his hands go up over everyone's heads in receiving a high corner kick, you will be able to readily see that they belong to the goalkeeper.

It may also be necessary for you and your partner to put on your striped shirts if an entire team or just the goalkeeper are wearing all black uniforms.

Needless to say, you must always have a change of uniform in your car in case this situation were to arise.

It is also very important that you learn to identify those people connected with each team, other than the uniformed players, so that you will be able to differentiate team personnel from spectators standing near the bench areas. This information is vital toward making the proper call involving dissent from those in the bench area.

Pre-Game Ceremony with the Captains

In conducting the pre-game ceremony with the captains, once again, greet them with a smile and introduce yourself. (Fig. 7) Encourage the opposing captains to shake hands and introduce themselves to each other, also. In your instructions, be concise and deliberate. Be prepared to cover those points important to you. Do not stammer trying to think of things to say. Get right to each point. Do not conduct a clinic or seminar on the rules of the game and soccer skills. Impress upon the captains that they have the responsibility of setting a good example for their teammates.

Do not forget to ask your partner if he would like to *add* anything different. That means that he should not repeat anything that you have said. Before the coin toss, be sure to ask the captains if they have any questions. This will assure you that all important points have been made as far as both officials and all of the captains are concerned. After the coin toss, it is also very important to remind the captains that they should go back to their teammates to tell them what was discussed and what will be expected of them by the officials. Many times, the captains keep all of your instructions to themselves and never inform their teammates and, sure enough, one or two calls during the game could have been prevented had the captains done their jobs properly.

Be certain to write down each captain's number. Do this so that the captain is aware of your recording his number. In fact, it would be wise to say, as you are writing, "Okay, captain Jones, your number is 14. Captain Smith, yours is 32". You do not have to explain why you are taking down their numbers because they will quickly realize that you are doing it in case you have to refer to them during the game. It will also place emphasis on your request that the captains set that good example for everyone else. Furthermore, if a player wishes to question one of your decisions, you will be able to tell quickly whether or not he is one of the captains.

Usually, in the coin toss, the visiting team captain is asked to call "heads" or "tails" while the coin is in the air. If it is foreign or an odd-looking coin, it would be wise to show the captains *before* the toss as to which side is considered "heads". If a team is represented by more than one captain, it behooves you to ask which one of them will be the spokesman.

Figure 7. Friendly Greeting for the Captains.

Figure 8. Coin Flip Alternative. In the absence of a coin, hide a blade of grass in either hand and ask the visiting captain to try to select the proper hand. If he guesses right, he has won the "toss".

Figure 9. Showing Everyone the Results of the Coin Toss. The captains should be told to face the direction in which their teams will be attacking in the first period.

If both officials have neglected to have a coin on hand, an alternative "coin toss" would be to pick up a small stone, a blade of grass or any small particle from the field and use it. You would simply show the item to the captains, then hide it behind your back while putting it into either hand. Then, after presenting both hands, fists closed, to the visiting captain, he is to select one of the hands. (Fig. 8) If he is correct, then he wins the "toss" and has the choice of kicking off or defending a goal. Naturally, if he selects the empty hand, then the home team has the choice.

Once the team captain, who has the choice to defend either goal or to kickoff, makes his decision, maneuver the two sets of captains around so that their backs will be facing the goal which they will defend in the first period. Then stand next to the captains of the team which will kickoff, face in the same direction that they are facing and make a kicking motion to indicate to everyone which team will kickoff and in what direction. (Fig. 9)

CHAPTER III

People Relationships

As a soccer referee, you come in contact with many different kinds of people. You must deal directly with the coaches and the players. You may deal directly with the spectators, but, for the most part, you will have more of an indirect relationship with them. You may have to deal with the host team manager if he is putting up the goal nets incorrectly; or the ticket taker at the stadium entrance if you are not in uniform and he asks for identification; or the custodian who has to let you back into the coach's office because you forgot something.

In dealing with each individual, it is vital that you be courteous but firm, friendly but not too friendly, authoritative but not dictatorial and decisive but not demeaning. You must be forever aware of the fellow officials whom you represent. Everything you do and everything you do not do must reflect favorably on you and your officials association.

The Referee-Coach Relationship

To get off on the right foot with a coach, greet him with a smile. To get off on the wrong foot with a coach, make demands on him as to how you are going to expect him to behave during the game. You should expect that he will conduct himself properly until he demonstrates otherwise. Any directive or anything that you might say to him before the game as to what he can and cannot do during the game will merely get you off on a negative note and he will resent it. If you look for trouble, you will be certain to find it.

It is very important that you do not allow yourself to treat a coach in any manner which would reflect upon an unpleasant incident which you may have had with him or his team in a previous game. Each game should be a

Figure 10. Giving the Coach a Private Warning.

new experience for you and the coach. You should not make any reference to the previous incident; in fact, it would be best for you to act as if you do not remember it or him at all and that, as far as you are concerned, you are meeting each other for the *first* time. In this manner, he should get the impression that you have either forgotten about the whole thing or have at least let bygones be bygones.

It will not take long for a coach to reveal how he will deal with and react to your calls, especially those which go against his team. If he begins to verge on negative or ungentlemanly conduct, try to work your way over to him during the next dead ball and tell him as privately (Fig. 10) as you can that you would like him to direct his comments toward his team only and not at you. (This would also apply if he has directed a derogatory comment toward your partner across the field. It will show him that you and your partner are working as a team.) Impress upon him the fact that he is one of the most influential people at the game and that it is most important to the success of the game that he set a good example for his players and his team's followers.

This private caution is a favor to him which he should appreciate. He should react accordingly. If he does not heed your advice, then you have no choice but to give him a yellow card for unsportsmanlike conduct or dissent on the next offense. In this manner, he cannot complain that he was not duly alerted to your feelings concerning his conduct.

The private caution is also the way to handle the coach who does not dissent with you directly but talks to his associates in a voice loud enough that you are certain to get his point. You may remind him that it is very difficult for you not to hear what he is saying and that if he wants you to do a good officiating job then he should let you concentrate on the game without having to listen to a great deal of bantering from the sidelines.

Another use of the private caution is to appeal to the coach to do something about one of his players who has become heated to the point where he is verging on dissent or violent conduct. Suggesting to the coach that he substitute for his player to give him a chance to settle down would not be over-stepping your bounds.

There will be moments when, during the half time interval, a coach (or spectator, usually a parent of one of the players) will approach you more than likely to question one of your calls or to get a rule interpretation. If you can readily see that he is a hostile visitor, it would be wise to greet him with a smile (introduce yourself if you have not done so already) and say "Yes, sir, what can I do for you?" This friendly greeting may help to neutralize the hostility that he has for you; then again, it may not.

Whatever he says, do not let it develop into a shouting match. You are certainly not going to yell at him and, of course, do not allow him to become highly vocal with you. Remember that you will probably be in the middle of the field at this time and everyone will be watching to see what happens. Answer his questions as well as you can, but do not let him dwell on something for which you have already given him a good explanation. Either walk away, or if it is close to the proper time, blow your whistle to get the second half started. If he persists in showing his dissent, give him a yellow card if he is a coach and order him back to his bench area or, in the case of an irate spectator, solicit the help of the appropriate coach.

In dealing with coaches, talk to them only when you have to. Many officials get into trouble by talking too much. You are a very important person out there. When you speak, people listen. But, just remember, what you say can and will be held against you. Be careful of what you say, and especially *how* you say it. You will be amazed as to how some people can so easily misinterpret what you have said by the tone of your voice.

The Referee-Player Relationship

Tone. What an interesting word. The motto to be followed in officiating any sport is: "Let your first few calls set the *tone* for the game." You must understand that, since the players have made an initial evaluation of you based upon what they saw you do and what they heard you say during the pre-game festivities, they will want to know what kind of a game you are going to call. Strict? Loose? In between? In actuality, they will know within a few minutes following the opening kickoff.

You must realize that "no-calls" are just as indicative as "calls". If there is a great deal of rough contact on an early play and you make no call, you have in essence set the tone for a very rough game. Furthermore, do not be foolish enough to think that the players will settle down later. To the contrary, they now know how much roughness you will allow and they also know that they will be able to challenge your consistency if you try to tighten up later in the game. It can be compared to the snow ball rolling down the hill—if you do not stop it right away, it will become an avalanche.

In dealing with the players, be firm but courteous. Your game vocabulary should always include, "sir", "please" and "thank you". Do not argue with anyone. It takes *two* people to make an argument. Keep a cool head. Never look down your nose at the players. Treat them with respect. As with the coaches, do not talk to them unless you must. Idle conversation with a player initiated by you will more than likely be misinterpreted by him as well as by nearby players from the opposing team. On the other hand, a good technique is to try to develop eye contact with each player at least once during the game. It will serve to show them that you are genuinely interested in their individual welfare.

If, during play, a push occurs which verges on being unsportsmanlike conduct, you should make the direct-kick call, but then add, "Come on, number 8, let's settle down, play that ball and not the man, I know that you don't want anybody to get hurt." — or any other type of cautioning phrase. Be sure, however, that your tone (there is *that* word again) of voice is more constructive than destructive.

All that players want from an official is consistency. Calls should be made in the same way no matter what the score is or how much time is left in the game. Your fellow officials also expect consistency from you. If you call a tight game at first, you should not loosen up later and vice versa.

If a player commits a cautionable offense, he should receive a yellow card. This should apply even if his team is ahead or behind by eight goals and there are only five seconds left on the clock. The players will appreciate it and the offending player will learn from it. If you do not make the call as it should be made, then you will simply be doing a disservice to the officials who are assigned to this player's next game. Most likely, the player will commit the same violation and when he gets yellow-carded he will retort, "I did the same thing in our last game and I didn't get a yellow card. How come you're giving me one now?" While you stand your ground with your yellow card in your hand, the player most certainly is grumbling in his mind, "Geez, these refs don't know whether they're coming or going — I don't know what to expect from them next."

As an official, you should refrain from addressing a male player as "Son". There are those players who would object to this for one reason or another. For example, there was the incident when a player was referred to as "Son" by the official and the player retorted, "Don't call me that; I'm not your 'son', plus I wouldn't want you to be my father". Needless to say, the official was rather stunned by the player's answer, but then he realized how negatively his reference had affected this player. Moral: If you must address a player in any manner other than by his number, be tactful.

The Referee-Spectator Relationship

When spectators are intent on cheering for their own team and leaving you and the other team alone, your job becomes much easier. However, when the crowd becomes unruly and unsportsmanlike, it makes for a long afternoon.

Some veteran officials say that the spectators should not bother you; that you should not hear them; that you should not wear "rabbit ears". For the most part, this is good, sound advice, especially at the college level and, maybe, at the high school level.

There are times, however, particularly during junior high and youth club games, that it pays to take the initiative when an individual insists on degrading you and what you stand for. This person might use foul and

Figure 11. **The Abusive Spectator.**

abusive language toward you. Sparing you the bad words, he might continually ride you on every call that you make. He is usually quite loud and most noticeable—normally by design. (Fig. 11)

While some officials would choose to ignore this individual and not react to him at all with the hopes that he will stop the abuse after seeing that his efforts are ineffective, others would take this opportunity to have that *private* chat with the coach whose team this person is supporting. The official's appeal to the coach would emphasize the point that he (the coach) is responsible for the conduct of his team's followers. In that vein, the coach should be asked to approach the agitator and remind him to set a good example for the youngsters at the game.

If the antagonist is allowed to carry on, he will rapidly lead the game into a state of deterioration. His negative attitude will have a direct effect upon other spectators at the game and soon they will join his bandwagon. And, of course, the players will pick up this tone (that word again) and begin to mouth off at each of your calls. Nip it in the bud. No one will fault you for trying to foster good sportsmanship in a game—no matter what the level of play.

There are times when the spectators vent their frustrations on the visiting team. For example, there was the junior high game in which one of the visiting players was having pebbles thrown at him from the students standing near the sideline. Another time, it was a player being shot at with rubber bands and paper clips. In both cases, the game must be stopped (preferably at the next dead-ball situation) and the home coach or a teacher from the host school summoned to take care of the culprits.

Occasionally, you will find that the players on the bench see themselves more as spectators than as players. Consequently, you hear "encouragement" being offered to their teammates on the field in the form of "Get that guy", "Cut him down", "Blast him", "Get him back". Once again, these comments will serve only to destroy the atmosphere of the game. You must address yourself to these players and remind them that they are not spectators and that you expect them to act as sportsmanlike players regardless if they are on the bench or on the field. A player on the bench is certainly not immune to being carded.

Many times, due to inadequate or non-existent barriers, spectators will be able to stand on the touch lines and the goal lines. With regard to those

Figure 12. Spectators Crowding the Touch Line.

along the touch lines, you should not say anything to them until the ball comes in their vicinity giving you the opportunity to see how they will react. (Fig. 12) If they move back quickly to avoid touching the ball while it is in play and if they give the player plenty of room to make his throw-in, then there is no need antagonizing them with a directive from you.

On the other hand, if the touch-line crowd shows a degree of unawareness of proper spectator etiquette, your best solution is to appeal to their common sense by saying, "Ladies and gentlemen, when the ball comes this way, please move back so that the players will have the opportunity to play the ball". If these spectators are reluctant to move when a player from the opposing team must make his throw-in their midst, you must come to his aid by announcing, "Please move back and give him room".

If the spectators are crowding the goal line and are standing behind the goal, it is imperative that these people be told, "Please join the side lines". (Fig. 13) There should be no opportunity for anyone to distract or aid the goalkeeper. This is simply good, sound preventive officiating. Once again, in making these directives to the spectators, it is most important that you be firm but courteous and always cognizant of the *tone* of your voice.

Figure 13. Spectators Behind the Goal. "Please join the side lines".

CHAPTER IV

Coordinating With Your Partner

Always respect your partner and his judgment. Never publicly criticize him even if it is two weeks later and you meet one of the coaches of that game at a social affair. It would be very easy to say to that coach, "Remember that partner I had in your game against Central? Boy, did he blow that one pushing call that cost your team the game." Pehaps it *was* a questionable call, but that is the way he saw it and that is why he called it. Your partner will not always agree with your calls either, but among the officals, *all* judgment calls should be supported now...and forever after.

It may happen during the game that your partner will make a call and a player nearby will say to you, "Man, that was a bum call". Your answer to him should be, "I thought it was a good call; besides he was closer to the play and had a better angle on it than you did". In this manner, players and coaches will begin to learn that the officials are out there as a team.

When it comes to rule interpretations, however, you must make sure that both of you, once again, as a team, are not credited with a misapplication of a rule. While you were supportive of each other's judgment, each of you must be certain that the rules are properly enforced in your game.

The following are common rule misapplications: (1) A *direct* free kick is awarded for dangerous play. (2) The ball, on a throw-in, is thrown parallel to the touch line and the wind blows it so that it never enters the field and the opposing team is awarded the ball because of an illegal throw in. (3) Play is allowed to continue when a player touches his teammate's goal kick before the ball has cleared the penalty area. (4) The goalkeeper is allowed to punt the ball out of the penalty area to restart play because he was holding it when the whistle was blown to stop play for an injured player up field.

Figure 14. Private Meeting of the Officials—away from the players in order to discuss a possible rule misapplication.

Rule misapplications should be prevented at all costs. But if one occurs, it should never be ignored with the hope that the players and coaches will not notice the mistake. While it may be embarrassing for you, or your partner, to correct a wrong doing, it will be worse if a player or coach brings it to your attention after you have tried to ignore it. Remember, it only takes one person in the crowd to recognize your mistake and you will have grief for the rest of the game if you do not correct it immediately.

If you detect a rule misapplication made by your partner, try to correct it on the spot and before he signals or blows his whistle to restart play. While it may be difficult to do it, you should blow your whistle to stop play, run toward your partner and beckon him to meet you halfway. Discuss the situation privately, away from all of the players. (Fig. 14) If you are the official who has made the mistake, then you are just going to have to be strong enough to admit it, express your regrets, rectify the situation and resume the game as quickly as possible. By all means, in correcting your partner's mistake, be certain to handle it in a manner whereby the players, coaches and spectators will maintain their respect for him as well as for you.

Be Alert to Your Partner's Decisions

The importance of blowing a sharp, loud whistle coupled with the appropriate signal cannot be overemphasized at this juncture. The field is large and crowd noise can be a problem in having your whistle heard not only by your partner but by all of the players as well. Secondly, your signals also inform everyone, including your partner, exactly what you have called.

The "no-call" signal (Fig. 15) should be honored by your partner. This signal, although unofficial, should be used when contact between two or more players is made (in your vicinity) which you feel is not deliberately caused by a player against his opponent. In essence, you are saying, "I have seen the contact, but I do not feel that a foul has been committed". This signal should be honored by your partner in that he should not make a call on this play. Actually, in doing so, he would be overruling your call since his call would involve blowing his whistle and stopping play.

This is not to say your partner cannot make a call in your area. It simply means that your "no-call" is a call in itself and it should be honored and not overridden. It should also be clear that a "no-call" and a "play on" (Fig. 15a) are two different things. In a "no-call" situation, a rule infraction has not occurred. In the "play on" instance, a violation of the rules has taken place, but the call is not made because in doing so you would penalize the team offended.

While using signals has been and will be emphasized here as a very important part of your performance as an official, there are times when not making a signal may be helpful later in the game. For example, what will you say

Figure 15. No-call Signal. A call in itself, it indicates that the official has seen the incident and has determined that no foul has occurred. This call should be honored by his partner and not overridden.

Figure 15A. Play-on Signal. This indicates that the official has seen a foul committed, but he does not blow his whistle, for, in doing so, he would penalize the team offended.

or signal when the ball goes over your touch line when you could not see who touched it last? This may happen two or three times per game.

If you have established a pattern of always pointing in the direction of the team which should throw in the ball, they will always be looking to you for this signal. Likewise, they will be listening for your voice if you have established a routine of always announcing the shirt color of the team which should throw in the ball. However, if, on plays when it is obvious to everyone who touched the ball last, you may choose not to make any manual or vocal signal. In this manner, later on when you are not sure who last touched the ball, you may be able to wait and let the players make the call for you. Usually, when a player causes the ball to go out of bounds, he will instinctively back off and move toward a defensive position. Similarly, one of his opponents will move toward the touch line to take the throw in. When this happens, you should merely point in the appropriate direction as if you had made the call yourself.

Naturally, the danger of this is when you have a player from each team going after the ball to take the throw in. One may genuinely believe that it is his team's throw in, while the other player is merely trying to influence your decision. When this happens and you honestly cannot make the call because you could not see who last touched it, you should look across to your partner. Your looking in his direction should immediately tell him that you need help in making the call.

If your partner has been observant, he should be able to give you an appropriate signal right away; usually by pointing in the direction of the team which he feels should be awarded the thrown-in. (Fig. 16) If he indicates that he does not know, then you have no choice but to declare a drop ball. At this juncture, you will not look too good; but if you express your regrets briefly and get two opponents together quickly, the oversight should be forgotten as soon as the ball is dropped and play resumes.

A point to be emphasized here is that the drop ball should not be made too close to the touch line or else you may find yourself in the same situation—the ball going out of bounds

Figure 16. **Signal Help from Your Partner.**

(off of the dropped ball) without your being able to tell who last touched it.

Another philosophy that may be applied to the situation in which you cannot detect who touched it last is that if you have been consistent in making decisive visual and verbal signals on each of your previous calls, chances are good that the players will readily accept your decision no matter which team it favors, even though it was a close play to call.

Lead and Trail System

In the dual-referee system, the officials usually cover the field in a lead and trail pattern, so that, during play, the lead referee is responsible for his nearest touch line and goal line, while the trail official is responsible for his nearest touch line and the half-way line. Being on opposite sides of the field, the officials automatically switch lead and trail responsibilities as the ball moves up and down the field. This coverage might be better understood if the areas of responsibility were designated as the right-front portion of the field for the lead referee and the left-rear portion for the trail referee. (Fig. 17) Keep in mind that, under certain association rules, the referees will switch at half time so that the lead referee will cover the left-front portion while the trail official will cover the right-rear area of the field.

In the right-front and left-rear trail alignment, the left-front and the right-rear portions of the field become difficult to cover because infractions which occur in these areas are as far from the lead referee as they are from

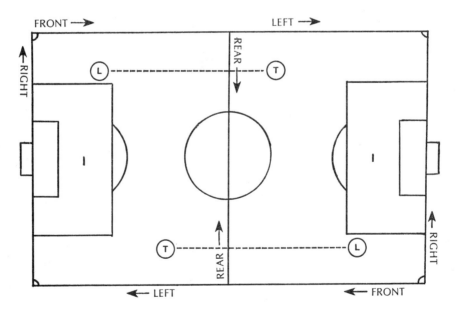

Figure 17. Lead and Trail Areas of Responsibility.

the trail referee. Consequently, these "coffin corner" calls—especially those in the left-front area—are some of the hardest calls to make, but they do not have to be if the two officials work together.

If the ball, for example, goes over the touch line near the left front corner flag, it can be very difficult for the trail official to ascertain this. However, if he notices that you, as the lead official, have not blown your whistle, it should indicate to him that you are waiting for him to blow his whistle to make the throw-in call. As lead referee, you can also help him by making a throw-in motion over your head. (Fig. 18) In this manner, you have helped him make the call.

Another problem which occurs frequently in the left front area is when the ball goes over the goal line and you, as the lead official, have had your view of the play blocked by the players in front of the goal. Since you are responsible for the goal-line calls, you must blow the whistle. The problem now is whether you award a goal kick or a corner kick. In most cases, your decision here will be crucial as many corner kicks lead to goals. Above all, you do not want to guess, and unless it is absolutely unavoidable, you do not want to call for a drop ball.

However, if you and your partner have pre-planned this system of helping each other, then all you have to do is blow your whistle (for the ball going over your goal line) and look to your partner. Hopefully, he has seen the

Figure 18. Help in Calling the Coffin-Corner Throw-in. The lead referee motions to tell his partner that the ball has gone out of bounds over his partner's touch line (and not the end line) near the flag in the coffin corner.

Figure 19. More Help in Making Coffin-Corner Calls. Having noticed that his partner needs help in making an end-line call in the coffin corner, the trail referee discretely points up field indicating that a goal kick should be signaled by the lead referee.

play. When he sees you looking toward him for help, he should discretely place his right or left forearm across his abdomen pointing either toward the corner (indicating a corner kick) or up field (indicating a goal kick). (Fig. 19) Upon receiving his signal, you should quickly make the appropriate signal as if it were your own call. This type of teamwork is very similar to the baseball plate umpire who looks to his base umpire for help as to whether or not the batter had completed his swing at a pitch.

Time Keeping

In most sections of the country and usually in games at the high school varsity and college levels, a timekeeper is provided by the home team and located at the timer's table at mid-field, between the two team benches. As the official, you must be certain that the timekeeper is knowledgeable on the rules of the game, especially with regard to when the clock is to be started and stopped. He must be made aware of your signals to indicate stoppage of the clock and under what conditions he is to resume running the clock.

The timekeeper must also be told what you expect of him in handling players entering the game as substitutes. He must know when substitutions may be made and he must have a signaling device (preferably a horn as opposed to a whistle) to use in order to get your attention before sending a substitute onto the field.

He must be instructed as to how to count out loud the last ten seconds of each period so that there will be no confusion on any goal or infraction which may occur as time expires. It is recommended that the timekeeper come out onto the field and remain close to the nearer official while announcing his countdown.

For games in which the officials are to keep the time on the field, it is best to designate one referee's watch as the official clock while the other referee runs his as a back-up clock in case the official clock becomes inoperative. It is also wise to let both coaches know which one of you has the official clock. If both team bench areas are on the same side of the field, it is best to have the referee nearer the benches running the official clock.

Some officials prefer to keep the time by saying "the first ref whose watch comes to the end of the period should blow his whistle." This is unwise because, while you may officiate 100 games without a close call to be made as time runs out, there will come that game when a goal is scored after one watch runs out and the other indicates a few more seconds are left in the period. What do you do then? Establish one watch as the official clock when neither one was so designated in the beginning? That would be very difficult to get across to a coach whose team had just lost the game because of that goal. In the system recommended, if referee "A" has the official clock, referee "B", when asked how much time is left, should simply answer, "Approximately 3½ minutes, but my partner has the official time."

Be sure to return your watch to zero after the end of the first half so that you can actually time the half-time interval. Otherwise, this interval could last longer than the allowable limit.

It is important to make sure that your partner is aware of how much time is left in each period when you have the official clock. Even though he has his watch running as a backup to yours, it is merely a good practice to let him know what the official clock says so that he can check his watch against yours. There is no need to alert him, however, until there are less than five minutes to go in the period.

You should develop the habit of always checking your watch, especially during these last few minutes, whenever there is a dead ball—usually when the ball goes out of bounds. Since there is, normally, a delay of a few seconds while the teams get set up for a goal kick, corner kick or throw in, this would be the time to signal to your partner how much time remains. Of course, he should be looking at you knowing that you will be giving him a time-check.

The time-check is best done by placing either hand over your abdomen with the appropriate number of fingers extended indicating the number of minutes left to play. (Fig. 20) To indicate half-minute intervals, you should make a plus sign with your hands. (Fig. 20a) Avoid giving these finger signals with your hand in the air, because, quite often, a multi-colored or congested background will make it difficult for your partner to determine the number of fingers which you have raised. (Fig. 21)

Just because a game is close as time is running out in a period, do not stop your clock for any reason (other than according to the rules) unless you have done so throughout the game. For instance, if the ball is kicked out of bounds and it will be a few more seconds than normal in retrieving it (in this case, no ball persons are provided because no extra game balls are available), do not stop the clock in an effort to save time when, earlier in the game, you did not stop the clock for the same type of delay. Be consistent in your timekeeping. You may choose to stop the clock, however, if the winning team begins to purposely kick the ball out-of-bounds in order to waste time. You should, of course, tell them what you are doing. Chances are good that they will then stop their time-wasting scheme.

After a Goal is Scored

After a goal has been scored, it is most important that the game be restarted without an unusual amount of delay. While the players on the team which scored are congratulating the shot-maker, it is recommended that the lead official, referee "A" in this case, retrieve the ball from the net.

Figure 20. Signaling a Time-Check to Your Partner. Three minutes to go in the period.

Figure 20A. Half-Minute Signal.

Figure 21. Raised Time Signals Difficult to Read—due to the congested background.

40

Do not wait for the opposing players to get the ball for you, because at this point, they are usually very disgruntled from being scored upon.

Referee "A" should then run with the ball toward the center circle and toss it to his partner, referee "B", who should be waiting at the mid-point of the half-way line. Tossing the ball from "A" to "B" should never exceed 15-20 yards and, of course, it should never be thrown in a manner whereby it might strike a player enroute. This is another reason for bringing the ball up field yourself, because many times, if the goalkeeper scored upon is allowed to send it up to the center circle, he will usually punt it aimlessly and, of course, the chances are good that it will land on somebody's head—a needless form of aggravation.

While "B" is placing the ball at mid-field for the ensuing kickoff, "A" should be taking his place on the half-way line near the touch line. "A" should then wait until "B" has moved to his lead position *and* has turned to face the center circle before blowing the whistle to restart play. It would also be wise and courteous for "A" to point to "B", a gesture which would mean, "Are you ready?" With "B" pointing up field, "A" would blow his whistle for the kickoff. All of this should be executed as quickly as possible. More importantly, the players should never have to wait for the officials to get the ensuing kickoff set up.

Since this ball-retrieving procedure is only a recommendation and not a mandatory procedure, there are those officials who oppose this technique. They feel that the scoring team should be allowed their moment of glory, while the team scored upon should be given a chance to recoup and regroup. The lead referee, in their opinion, should be unobtrusively returning to the half-way line for the kickoff. It is felt that, by entering the goal-mouth area and seeking the ball, the referee loses a degree of dignity and, at the same time, gives the team scored upon an opportunity to complain or protest the call. No matter with which philosophy you and your partner agree, it must be done similarly by each of you throughout the game.

More often than not, coaches make multiple substitutions immediately after a goal is scored. In games without a timekeeper's table, coaches tend to make these substitutions without formally getting the referee's attention. This can be prevented by a reminder to each coach before the game. Furthermore, you should expect substitutions to be made at this time and, therefore, you should be looking toward the bench areas before blowing the whistle for the kickoff.

CHAPTER V

Mechanics

If an official is on top of the play and has a clear view of the action, there should be no complaints. This means RUN, HUSTLE. An official should be able to anticipate things that will happen and, therefore, be in the proper position to make the call. Another motto which prevails here is, "Presence lends conviction".

As the lead referee, you should move into the vincinity of the penalty area when the ball is being played near the goal mouth. (Fig. 22) And when a shot is taken, you must be on or very near the goal line so that you will be in a good position to tell whether or not the ball has completely crossed the line. While no one will argue the point when the ball reaches the back of the net, your call becomes very critical when the goalkeeper bobbles the ball near the line or when the ball caroms downward off the crossbar and bounces on or near the line. You will satisfy no one if you are out by the 18-yard line trying to make your decision.

Do not watch the ball while it is in the air. Do not "skylark". There will be nothing happening around the ball. All of the action—holding, pushing, obstruction, etc.—will be taking place on the ground below the ball. The only time you should concern yourself with the ball in flight is when it may go completely out of bounds while in the air. Similarly, you should occasionally look "off the ball", that is, watch the action between two players *after* the ball has left their area.

How and When to Blow that Whistle

An official should blow a sharp, crisp, loud whistle on most calls. However, on out-of-bounds calls when it is obvious that the ball has gone

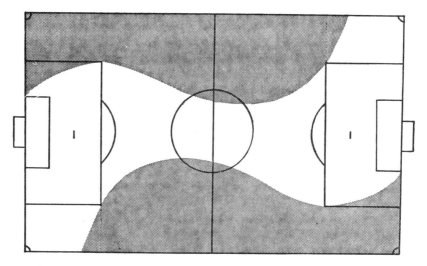

Figure 22. **Cutting the Corner. When the Ball is in the area of the goal mouth, the lead referee should move in to cover the action.**

well over the line, a short, brisk whistle is all that is necessary. On the other hand, there may be times when an extra loud whistle can be used to make a point, such as in preventing a fight or prior to issuing a yellow or red card. You should realize that the manner in which you blow your whistle, many times, reflects the manner in which you would speak if you did not have use of a whistle. It can be used very effectively in making your calls.

In restarting play, after a dead ball situation, you may or may not blow your whistle. It lies within your discretion. You are, however, expected to blow your whistle to signal for a kickoff and a penalty kick to be taken. You should also blow it to restart play after a substitution has been completed. On all other free kicks, corner kicks, goal kicks, throw-ins or drop balls, the players need not wait for a whistle unless you have specifically requested that they wait for you or your partner's whistle.

Making Calls and Using Signals

One of the most important factors in a well-officiated game is how you keep the game under control. In all sports, the officials must be decisive authoritative and convincing. He must make certain that everyone—the players, coaches and spectators—knows exactly what has been called on each infraction. While they might not always agree, they will, at least, know that you are not afraid of making a call.

Call only that which you actually see. If a player inadvertently blocks you from seeing an infraction, you have no business trying to call it. If you miss it, chances are that your partner will catch it and he should make the call. That is one of the values of the dual-referee system. On the other hand, if both of you see an infraction and blow your whistles simultaneously, one of you should give in to the other so that only one call is made. You should agree prior to the game on what your course of action will be if this happens. Perhaps the official farther from the incident than his partner will yield to his partner's decision.

Once again, your tone in making calls cannot be overemphasized. It is not necessarily what you say that is most important, but rather *how* you say it. A good way to avoid being misinterpreted is to let your whistle and hands convey the messages. On the other hand, maintaining control of the game and keeping everyone informed of what is going on are best achieved by the official who signals and announces *all* of his calls. This applies at the youth club level through collegiate play.

Many times, your signals may have to be less official and more demonstrative in order to get your point across. For example, if a player raises his forearm to his side and away from his body to ward off an attacking player, he should be called for pushing or, more than likely, holding. Unfortunately, the official signals do not describe that infraction very accurately and, therefore, it would be more helpful to everyone if you were to give the proper signal supplemented by your *imitation* of the infraction. (Fig. 23)

Imitations of rule violations by the official can also be very educational to the players. For instance, it would be considered good preventive officiating if you, in calling an illegal throw-in, would imitate what the player did wrong. You should lift one foot to the rear to indicate that both feet were not on the ground at the time of throw, or you should imitate the ball being thrown over the shoulder, as opposed to over the head, to demonstrate that infraction. (Fig. 24) Not only will this gesture bolster your rapport with the players showing your sincere concern for their skill development, it should also cut down on the number of throw-in violations during the remainder of the game.

If you choose not to tell the player what he did wrong, he will, more than likely, make the same mistake repeatedly. Sooner or later, he will become frustrated and retort harshly, "What was wrong with it"? Then you have a situation which verges on dissent with the official and, possibly, a yellow card being issued. All of this could have been avoided had you chosen to correct his mistake in the first place.

In making your verbal calls, be sure that you are brief and to the point. No one wants to listen to you present a long oratory on his shortcomings. Always speak in terms of a team's shirt color and never by the name of the team or school. Furthermore, while a team's shirts may be maroon or yellow, it is better to use one-syllable words and call them "red" or "gold", respectively.

Figure 23. Signaling by Imitating the Infraction. Supplementing the imitation signal with the standard signal would be more completely descriptive of the incident.

Figure 24. Demonstrating Illegal Throw-ins. In this manner, the players will learn from their mistakes.

On an out-of-bounds call along the touch line, simply announce "red" indicating the team which is to take the throw-in. This call should be supplemented by extending your arm parallel to the ground and pointing in the direction which the red team is attacking. As indicated previously, the verbal call can be omitted most of the time in favor of the directional signal only. However, there are times, usually when the teams have just switched ends of the field, when you temporarily lose track of which direction a team is attacking; therefore, it would be better to announce the shirt color rather than point in the wrong direction. A common fault on touch line calls is for the official to say, "Out on blue, red throw-in". First of all, all of that verbiage is unnecessary and secondly, telling them that it is a "throw-in" is virtually insulting the players' intelligence.

When two opponents touch the ball *almost* simultaneously before it caroms off of one player's foot and goes out of bounds, it is wise to give a supplementary signal to indicate this. This is simply done by lifting your foot and sweeping your hand across it, demonstrating the tipped ball and the reason for your call. (Fig. 25) In the minds of some distant spectators and players, the thrown-in should have gone the other way—your tipped-ball signal helps to explain your call.

On the calls which are made during play, such as pushing, holding, handling the ball, dangerous play and obstruction, a four-part announcement supplemented with the appropriate signals will be all encompassing and informative to everyone who can hear you and see you. "Pushing white, orange direct"; "Obstruction green, gold indirect", are examples.

After you have blown the whistle to stop play and you have waited a

Figure 25. Signaling a Tipped Ball—showing the reason for his call, as it may not have been detected by those watching at a distance.

moment to give everyone a chance to turn toward you (some officials make their calls and signals so fast that most players miss them), give the infraction first—"Obstruction" followed by the shirt color—"green"—of the team causing the violation. When the green players hear their shirt color, they will begin moving toward their defensive positions. During both of these parts of your call, you should be making your signal for obstruction. (Fig. 26) Next, you indicate "gold", which is the team to take the kick and what type of kick, "indirect", it is to be. During these statements, you should be giving the two-arm signal for an indirect kick and pointing both arms in the direction that the gold team is attacking. (Fig. 26a)

Figure 26. Parts One and Two of the Four-Part Call. "Obstruction, Green...", coupled with the signal.

Figure 26A. Parts Three and Four of the Four-Part Call. "...Gold, Indirect,"—again with the signal.

If you wish to be more particular or if you want to make sure that the player guilty of the violation knows it, you could say, "Tripping, red 17, blue direct". This not only impresses number 17 to be more cognizant of his style of play, but it also shows everyone else, especially his coach, that you know exactly who committed the violation.

Even if you do not announce the guilty player's number, you should still know what it is. Many times, a coach will yell out to you, "Who'd you call that on"? Needless to say, it sounds much more impressive and convincing if you are able to say, "Number 17, coach", rather than to stammer and reply, "Well, uh, I think it was one of your midfielders, coach".

In using your hand signals for direct and indirect free kicks, keep in mind that not very many players recognize the difference between the two signals. (Whenever you have the opportunity to describe the difference, point out that the *two*-armed signal means that *two* players must touch the ball before a goal can be scored.) They would much rather hear it from you, especially when a goal is imminent. However, since both words are very similar, it is important that no one be confused as to which word you have said. It is recommended that you place the emphasis on the first syllable. Say "DYE-rect" and "INN-di-rect". As a reminder, the lead official should be giving this command when a shot-on-goal is probable so that everyone, especially the kicker and the goalkeeper, will know exactly what type of kick it will be.

Another similarity, which may cause confusion, is with the direct and in-direct signals themselves. For example, when a player faces your left side and he sees that your left arm is hanging down normally but your right arm is extended at shoulder level and in a forward direction, he recognizes the direct-kick signal very easily. However, if both of your arms are raised for an indirect kick, your left arm may be blocking his view of your right arm caus-ing him to interpret your signal as one calling for a direct kick. (Fig. 27) This problem can be avoided when giving the indirect kick signal by pointing one arm about 10° *above* the parallel-to-the-ground position, and pointing the other 10° *below* the level position. This should enable players with a side view of your signal to readily see that *both* arms are extended in a forward direction. (Fig. 27a) It is also recommended that both referees continue to display their kick signals until the ball is put into play and, in the case of an indirect kick, until a second player has touched the ball.

Unfortunately, at this writing, no official signal has been designated by the NCAA when a "goal kick" is the call. Consequently, there are several dif-ferent signals which are currently being used by officials.

Normally, the lead referee, who would blow his whistle and make the goal kick signal, is facing the penalty area when giving this signal. One signal be-ing used is when the referee extends his left arm to his side, parallel to the

Figure 27. Deceptive and Distinct Indirect Kick Signals. In this view of the official on the left, it is difficult to tell whether or not his right arm is also raised. (It is!) There is no question with the signal being given on the right.

Figure 28. Confusing and Unnecessary Goal-Kick Signals. The pointing of the right hand toward the goal area is unnecessary since the players know that that is where the ball is to be placed for a goal kick. The signal on the right could be easily confused as one calling for a corner kick in the coffin corner.

ground as to point up field, while extending his right arm to his front, parallel to the ground as to point toward the goal area. (Fig. 28) Another similar signal used involves the left arm doing the same thing while the right arm is directed downwards at about 45° as if it were pointing to the spot in the goal area where the kick is to be taken. (Fig. 28)

A third signal used is when the left arm is hanging normally while the right arm is pointing toward the goal area. (Fig. 28) This one is not recommended because it is virtually identical to the signal which you would use in calling for a corner kick at the left front corner.

The former two signals are not recommended either because with the right arm pointing toward the goal area, it is, once again, insulting to the player's intelligence. That is to say that if you are signaling for the kick to be taken up field, as in a goal kick, there is no need telling the players where to place the ball, except when the ball goes directly over the center of the goal. Furthermore, the right arm signal once again, looks very much like a signal for a corner kick.

When the ball goes over the goal line, one of only three signals can be given. Since the signal for a goal scored (both arms extended straight up) is most distinguishable and the right arm is pointed to the appropriate corner for a corner kick, it is recommended that only the left arm be used in indicating a goal kick. The arm should be extended to the side, parallel to the ground as if to point in the direction the kick is to be taken. (Fig. 29) This gives the official three signals, each very distinguishable from the others, to use when making calls at the goal line.

It is important to remember, however, that the indirect kick signal be used before the goal kick is taken. Even though a score is unlikely directly from a goal kick, you should still make the proper signal.

For the same reasoning, it is also wise to make the indirect kick signal when blowing the whistle for a kickoff and to make the direct kick signal just prior to a corner kick. You should never assume that the players know what kind of kicks these are. A player, especially a goalkeeper who has just been scored upon, should never be able to say, "But you never indicated what kind of a kick it was supposed to be."

Pointing your signals in the proper direction is relatively simple on goal kicks, corner kicks and kickoffs. However, when making calls for throw-ins and free kicks, it is not as easy to determine a team's direction of attack as quickly as you should in order to make your signal understandable and smooth-flowing.

There are, probably, as many ways to keep track of a team's direction as there are officials working games. Some look back quickly, while making a call, to see the shirt color of the fullbacks to determine in which direction their team is going. Another way is to, at the beginning of each period, repeatedly say to yourself, "Blue is my team. Blue is my team." This may mean the team attacking toward you or away from you. Either way makes no difference. You should use whatever method is best for you to quickly determine a team's direction.

Your decision as to which team should take a throw-in, many times can be aided by your pointing in the *opposite* direction that the ball was heading as it went out of bounds. (Fig. 30) That is to say that, about nine times out of ten, the ball, as it goes over the touch line, has been last touched or kicked by a player whose team is attacking in the same direction as the ball was traveling. By simply pointing in the opposite direction, you have made a quick and accurate call. Suffice to say, you must be alert for those few times when the ball goes out in the opposite direction of a team's attack.

Employing the correct directional signal on a throw-in is very important as many leagues use the rule by which substitutions are allowed by a team on their own throw-in. Naturally, if the team bench is across the field from you and the coach wants to make a substitution, you will help him tremendously by making the proper directional signal. Announcing only a shirt color will merely delay the game because the coach, unable to hear your call, will not ask to send in a substitute until he sees that one of his players is given the ball for the throw-in. Sometimes the throw-in happens so quickly, that, if you have not signaled properly, the coach may miss this opportunity to substitute and he will become disgruntled with you because of it.

When you are the official timekeeper and will be blowing the whistle to signify the end of a period, be sure to hold your watch up at eye level so that you will be able to see the game action behind it, especially in the last five seconds. In this manner, you will be able to determine exactly where the ball is as time runs out. It is also most important that you have your whistle in your mouth so that you will be able to blow it loud and clear as the second hand hits zero.

Once you have blown your whistle announce, "Halftime". "Game", "Quarter" or whatever is appropriate as you are making the time-out signal. Some officials blow an extra long, wailing-type whistle and say nothing nor give any signal. In this manner, it takes a few seconds for everyone to realize the purpose of the whistle. This is unnecessary. People should never have to guess as to what an official has called, to include the end of a period.

In reading and studying the NCAA rulebook, you will note that it states, "...kick, strikes, attempts to kick or strike..trips, or attempts to trip..." It is very easy for an official to overlook the word "attempts" and subsequently not enforce it in the game. Some officials prefer to call nothing just because there was no contact or because the player was unsuccessful in attempting to kick, strike or trip an opponent. By not penalizing this player and calling for a direct kick, the official is actually helping to nurture a rough game and

Figure 29. Recommended Goal-Kick Signal. This signal indicates the direction the kick is to be taken. More importantly, it cannot be confused with a corner-kick signal nor the signal for a goal.

Figure 30. Determining a Team's Direction for a Throw-in. Pointing in the *opposite* direction of the path of the ball as it goes out of bounds affords you a quick signal in 90% of your touch-line calls. However, watch out for that 10%!

an unhealthy atmosphere. A yellow card, for unsportsmanlike conduct, might also be appropriate in this case.

Unless most of the spectators, coaches and players at your game are knowledgeable of the rules and considerate of your task, you will, more than likely, have 50% of these people agreeing with each of your calls, while the other half will not. This is to be expected and, in most cases, should be ignored. You should definitely not be bothered by a negative reaction when you feel that you were in a good position to make the call and that you used your best judgment. After all, that is what you are out there for—to use your judgment.

There will be times, however, when players, coaches and even spectators, will question your call, not in a belligerent or demeaning manner, but with a degree of concern that perhaps the wrong decision was made. If you see or hear this type of reaction, think it over. Be sure you are correct. Ask your partner what he saw. Remember that he will not make the call unless you ask him to, or unless he recognizes that you have missapplied a rule as we discussed earlier. If you are wrong, do not be afraid to reverse your decision. You gain the respect of everyone if you do everything possible to make certain that all calls are made in accordance with the rules.

Review this actual incident: In a 15-and-under girls' club game, a strong, driving shot was taken toward the upper left corner of the goal. The goalkeeper made a desperate and courageous leap for the ball and successfully tipped it over the crossbar. Upon landing hard on the turf, however, the goalkeeper doubled up having had the wind knocked out of her. At first, all of the players, coaches and spectators were ecstatic with her great save, giving her a standing ovation. Naturally, this subsided as soon as they saw that she was hurt. After a considerable delay, while the coaches attended the injured goalkeeper, the lead official was ready to restart play. However, in getting caught up with the emotion surrounding the play and the subsequent injury, he incorrectly signaled for a goal kick. Since the flow of the game was abruptly stopped by the injury, the official had not given any signal or made any call other than to blow the whistle to stop play.

As soon as the goalkeeper had recovered and was ready to play, the goal kick signal was given. Both teams reacted accordingly without any of them recognizing the discrepancy. In fact, not until the goal kick was taken and the ball was in the air, did the official hear someone behind him say, "Hey, ref, shouldn't that have been a corner kick?" Quickly, the referee reconstructed the play in his head and realized his mistake. Just as quickly, he reacted by blowing the whistle, stopping play and announcing for all to hear, "I'm sorry, but that should have been a corner kick. Remember how the goalkeeper tipped the ball?"

Now this is a case where the official could have very easily let it slide because none of the players, the coaches nor even his partner realized what had happened. Furthermore, the rules stipulate that, once play has resumed, a call should not be reversed. But because someone noticed it and let it be known, the official chose to bring the play back and restart play as it should have been.

The real test of this official's integrity and desire to make a call properly would have presented itself if absolutely no one, other than himself, had detected the wrong decision. Would he have stopped play in a similar fashion and admit to everyone that he had made a mistake, or would he have just let it go hoping that no one would bring it up later? This is were one's conscience enters the picture. Could you live with yourself later after not having rectified the situation at the time? This is a question only you can answer for yourself.

Game Delays, Injuries and Restarts

If you must stop the game for an injured player while the ball is in play, you should blow your whistle, signal timeout, stop your watch and beckon the player's coach or trainer to attend to the injury. You should then immediately announce to all of the players, "We'll restart with a drop ball over there", pointing to the spot where the ball was when play was suspended. If time is halted for an injury after the ball has gone over the touch line, the same procedure should be used, however, in this case, the call should be, "We'll restart with a blue throw-in".

In making this restart-procedure announcement immediately, it alerts all of the players so that they will be able to plan any strategy which they might have in mind. More importantly, however, it will prevent anyone from complaining to you to the contrary in the event that a long delay causes some people to forget what was happening when play was stopped to attend to the injured player.

If at all possible, you should avoid having to stop play for an injured player while the ball is in the penalty area. It is important to attend to the injured player as quickly as is feasible, but you should say to yourself, "I recognize the injured player, and I also see that the goalkeeper is about to punt the ball up field. If I wait two seconds to give him a chance to punt it out of the penalty area, I can merely blow the whistle while the ball is in the air, causing a drop-ball restart somewhere up field. This would prevent having to call for a drop-ball restart at the nearest spot outside the penalty area (NCAA rules) or inside the penalty area (FIFA rules)."

If you feel that the injury is so serious that you cannot wait for the goalkeeper to get rid of the ball you should stop play immediately, have the injured player attended to and conduct the drop-ball restart in accordance with the rules in effect. Naturally, the goalkeeper will contend that he should still be able to punt the ball, because, in essence, the injured player is taking the advantage away from him. While it may be a sensible argument, the drop ball is the only restart procedure to be used in this case under NCAA rules. (National High School Federation rules are different and allow the team in possession to restart play with an indirect kick).

Upon recognizing an injured player, usually one who is on the ground in noticeable pain, you must must first check the flow of play before blowing your whistle to stop the game. If the ball is merely being played back and forth between the two 18-yard lines, play should be stopped immediately to attend to the injured player. However, if either team is on the offensive with a solid attack in progress, for the protection of the game, play should be allowed to continue until the ball goes out of play, a violation occurs or the attack is thwarted.

You will be protecting the game because you will not allow an injured player, perhaps one who is faking an injury, to prevent his opponents from completing a potential scoring play. On the other hand, you must be cognizant of the possibility of a player being injured further or more seriously if play is allowed to be continued too long before attending to him. It is recommended that you move toward the injured player to get a better idea of the extent of the injury. Let the player know that you are aware of his situation. Furthermore, you should protect him in case the ball were to quickly change direction and place the injured player in a vulnerable position. By this time, however, play should be stopped.

In the same vein, you should be very careful not to intervene in the on-the-field treatment of an injured player. This responsibility should rest with the player's coach or trainer, or parents, if they are present. You should, however, be helpful if no responsible person is knowledgeable enough to know what to do or what not to do. In most cases of a serious injury, especially those in which the victim displays a great deal of pain, the recommended procedure would simply be to keep the victim still and warm and immediately call for the local rescue squad or similar agency.

Remember to beckon the coach or trainer onto the field. While most of them will be running onto the field before you ask them to, there are others who will wait for your signal. Needless to say, it would be most embarrassing if a coach had to remind you to let him attend to his player.

During the game, there may be a case when you recognize an injured player, allow the attack to continue and in that time-period blow your whistle for a tripping violation. In this situation, play is stopped, the injured player should be attended to and the game should be restarted with a direct kick by the team whose player was tripped. The fact that the player was injured prior to the violation is not a factor in the restart procedure because you did not officially recognize the injury by blowing your whistle for it.

Having a drop ball in this case, instead of awarding a direct kick for the tripping violation, would be a misapplication of the restart rule.

Making Substitutions

For games in which you have personnel manning the timer's table, it is imperative that both team benches be on the same side of the field as the timer. If a coach insists that his bench area be placed on the opposite side, perhaps to have his team seated in front of his spectators, then this coach must understand that his substitutes will have to go around the field in order to check in with the timer.

The timer's sounding device must be strong enough to get the attention of nearer official. Substitutes must be recognized and beckoned onto the field by the referee and they must enter the field from the timer's table. Players, checking in with the timer to go in as substitutes, must remain at the table and may not return to their bench in order to enter the field from there. You must make sure that your timer understands and enforces this policy.

You should also instruct the coaches to have their substitutes checked in and ready at the table so that there will be a minimal delay when the appropriate substitution time arises.

When your game is without a sideline timer, you must make it clear to both coaches as to how you expect substitutions to be made. No matter if the team benches are on the same or opposite sides of the field, a coach, wishing to make a substitution, should merely have to announce to the official nearer to him "Ref, Sub".

Upon hearing the coach's request, you must be certain that it is the proper time for substitution. If so, you should blow your whistle with several (4 to 6) short blasts and raise one hand (straight up with fingers extended) to notify your partner of the substitutions about to be made. You should then signal with your other hand, the player(s) to enter the field with a beckoning motion, similar to a traffic policeman (Fig. 31). Coaches and players must understand that substitutions cannot be made until the referee recognizes the players coming into the game.

Some coaches prefer to wear a whistle of their own and blow it whenever they want to make a substitution. This practice should not be permitted because of the chance that a coach will blow his whistle at the wrong time. A typical example is when a kick, taken by the offensive team, goes over their opponent's goal line. It looks like a simple goal kick. On the play, however, the lead referee detects obstruction and that is why he has blown his whistle, and not because of the ball going out-of-bounds. While the referee is clearly making the proper signal, the coach, hearing only the whistle, misses the signal as he is busily getting his substitutes ready to go into the game. Consequently, when the coach blows his whistle, he must be cor-

Figure 31. Beckoning Substitutes into the Game.

rected publicly and, naturally, he will be somewhat embarrassed by it. This could be avoided by not allowing him to use his whistle in the first place. Before the game, you should notice if either coach is wearing a whistle around his neck.

When accepting substitutions into the game, it is very important that the two referees work harmoniously. If, on a goal kick called by you as the lead referee, the coach on your side of the field tells you that he wants to make a substitution, you should blow your 4 to 6 short blasts on your whistle, raise one hand and beckon them in with the other. Just as importantly, however, you should tell the player about to take the goal kick to wait for your whistle (NCAA) or command (FIFA). This will prevent the kick from being taken prematurely and while the substitutions are being made.

When it is your partner's goal kick or corner kick and the coach yells, "Ref, Sub", merely give those short blasts on your whistle to alert your partner, raise your hand and beckon them in. However, it is most important that you keep your hand raised until all of the substitutions have been completed. In this manner, your partner will simply need to watch you and not restart play until you have lowered your hand and beckoned to him accordingly.

The illegal-substitution call should be made only if a coach is caught trying to sneak a player onto the field during play. At all other times, that is, in dead-ball situations, the coach cannot possibly make an illegal substitution because a substitute is not a player until you have beckoned him onto the field. If the coach calls out, "Ref, Sub", and has his player running onto the field before you can indicate to him otherwise, merely send the player back to the bench and announce to the coach, "Sorry, Coach, no subs now, it's a drop ball." (Or whatever the inappropriate instance might be.)

If the coach or his players neglect to inform you or your partner that they are putting in a new goalkeeper, you may want to say to that coach, as discretely as possible, "Say, Coach, are you changing goalkeepers?" He will probably reply, "Oh, yeah, right, I was just about to let you know", or something like that. You may also choose to simply recognize the substitute's different-colored shirt, beckon him in and announce to your partner, "Bill, new goalkeeper."

This gesture would be considered by some referees as good preventive officiating, while others would contend that you have overstepped your bounds and are coaching. Perhaps it would be appropriate at lower levels where inexperienced coaches are prevalent, but not on the upper levels where a better knowledge of rules is to be expected. As long as you and your partner would act uniformly there should be no harm in it. Certainly, the coach, having received the reminder, would appreciate it greatly and learn by it.

It should be emphasized, however, that once an official has been informed of the goalkeeper change, he must notify his partner immediately. This, of course, would prevent an uninformed official from making an illegal substitution call as soon as the "illegal" goalkeeper touches the ball.

On the Kickoff

The official who places the ball on the half-way line and in the center of the circle for the kickoff shall become the trail official as soon as the ball is put into play. From his position on the half-way line and just outside of both wing players, he is responsible for making sure that all of the players are on their own side of the half-way line and the ball is stationary. He should also check to see that both goalkeepers are ready, especially the kickoff team's opposing goalkeeper. At the beginning of each period, it is wise to check with both goalkeepers by asking each one, "Goalkeeper, ready?" (Some officials do this after each goal, but it is not recommended.) Naturally, the official should wait for each goalkeeper to respond with an appropriate signal or answer. He should also check to see that his partner is ready. Once all is in order, the trail official should blow his whistle sharply so that all players will be alert to the ball being put into play.

The ball is in play as soon as it has traveled at least 27 inches in a forward direction while being touched by only one player. The trail official is responsible that these criteria be met. If the ball is not kicked into the opponent's half of the field or if it does not travel at least 27 inches before being played again, the whistle should be blown and the kickoff retaken. Furthermore, to help prevent a repeat of the same infraction, the trial official should announce to the players a directive such as, "Remember, the ball must go forward on a kickoff". (Another example of preventive officiating.)

The trail official, after he has blown his whistle for the kickoff, must also make certain that all of the players remain in their own half of the field until the ball is put into play. Some players will often move across the line on the whistle rather than wait for the ball to be kicked. If this happens, the trail official should blow his whistle, call for the kick to be retaken and remind the offenders of the proper procedure.

Once the ball has been put into play, the trail official must also watch that the player taking the kick does not play it again before it is touched by any other player. If this should occur, their opponents would be awarded an indirect free kick at the point of the infraction.

The lead official, prior to the kickoff, places himself outside the players on his side of the field and about 15 yards downfield, that is, that half of the field into which the kick will be taken. (Fig. 32) His main responsibility is to ensure that all defensive players remain outside of the center circle until the ball is put into play. Upon seeing this infraction, he should blow his whistle and call for the kick to be retaken. Furthermore, he should be alert for any other infraction which his partner might miss.

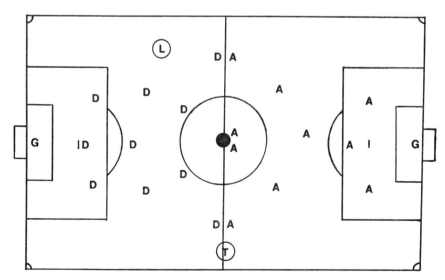

Figure 32. **Positioning of Officials on a Kickoff.**

Free Kicks

Besides throw-ins, the call made most frequently during a game is that which results in a free kick. In view of this, it is important that you know your direct-kick offenses from your indirect-kick offenses. There is no excuse for calling "dangerous play" and then awarding a direct kick.

Under current NCAA rules, you are expected to blow your whistle to restart play prior to a kickoff and a penalty kick and after a substitution has been made. On all other kicks, a player merely needs to place the ball onto the appropriate spot and make sure that it is stationary before putting it back into play.

If, however, you are working a game in which the rules require the use of a restart whistle on all kicks, you must always be alert so that the player taking the kick should never have to wait for your whistle. This is particularly critical on a violation for which you have awarded a team a free kick and that team wishes to get the ball back into play before their opponents have a chance to get back on defense. It is a smart play, but you will be unimpressive when your delayed whistle prevents them from carrying out their strategy. Once you have blown your whistle for the violation and given the appropriate signal, you should blow your second whistle as soon as you see that the ball is ready for play.

Be certain not to allow the ball to be played while the ball is moving. If you have blown your whistle, you will be forced to call for the kick to be retaken. Naturally, the kicker will justifiably retort with, "Well, I kicked it because you blew the whistle". In essence, he would be correct and nothing you could say would alleviate this embarrassing moment except to admit your error and get on with the game as quickly as possible.

It is very important to remember that on all free kicks, the ball is not in play until it has traveled the distance of its own circumference—at least 27 inches. (Exception: When a goal kick or any free kick is taken by the defensive team from within their own penalty area, the ball is not in play until it has completely gone over the penalty area line.) While it does not happen very often, if a player, taking a free kick, were to play the ball twice *before* it has traveled at least 27 inches, it would not be a violation, but simply a rekick because the ball had not yet been put into play.

In keeping with this, many times when a team has been awarded an indirect free kick in or near their opponent's penalty area, the kicker would approach the ball, as if to kick it, but merely step on it. It would be his feeling that he has played it once, thus allowing a teammate to follow immediately behind him taking a hard shot-on-goal. This shot should not be allowed because the ball had not rolled its circumference and it would have been considered to have been moving when the ball was put into play. The indirect free kick, however, should be retaken with the appropriate explanation given to the players.

The thumb rule to follow on free kicks is that only the kickoff and penalty kick must be kicked in a forward direction. Nevertheless, it should also be noted that "forward" includes any of the 179° in front of the spot where the ball rests.

A fairly common play which should not come as a surprise to you is when the goalkeeper allows an indirect kick to go untouched into his goal net. It is obviously no goal because it was not touched by any other player and it should simply be called a goal kick for the defensive team as a result of the ball going over the goal line by the offensive team.

Quite often, players on the defensive team will form a human wall to help protect their goal when a score is imminent from a free kick. However, in setting up their wall, they invariably place themselves less than the prescribed ten yards away from the ball. They do this, many times, to try to gain an advantage hoping that you will let them get away with it, or they are merely delaying the game so that the rest of their defense will have a chance to set up. You must be on the top of this immediately. On the first few free kicks of the game, the players must be aware of the fact that you will not tolerate any delay tactics such as these. Making this point with the captains in your pre-game conference will also help prevent this type of play which detracts from the spirit of the game.

You need not pace off the ten yards. Actually, in doing so, you are helping the defensive team in their ploy to delay the game. Instead, with a good, firm command, you should tell them to move as far as you feel they should be in order to comply with the rule. (Fig. 33)

You should also remember that the ten-yard rule applies to the kicker's opponents in 360 directions around the ball. There are times when a defensive player will try to stand behind the kicker and within the ten-yard radius to gain an advantage in case the kicker plays the ball to a nearby teammate rather than kick it straight ahead. You must watch this player also and prevent him from carrying out his scheme.

There are other times when a defensive player will blatantly stand directly in front of the ball in order to delay the kick so that his players can set up a better defense. This player must be dealt with quickly and severely. The rules stipulate that this is unsportsmanlike and a yellow-card offense. Therefore, you should react accordingly. By the same token, if the players, in setting up the human walls as discussed above, do not properly respond to your directive to move back, then the only appropriate action you have is to issue a yellow card to the player or players guilty. Once again, setting this tone early in the game is most critical to the flow of the game in its later stages.

In getting into position, as the lead official, when it is your responsibility to watch the wall, it is vital that you be off to the side and slightly behind the

Figure 33. Getting That Wall of Players Back Ten Yards. Refrain from pacing it off. When *you* say it's ten, it's ten.

wall. Being even with the wall affords a good view of offside, but being slightly behind the wall also allows you to catch the holding or pushing violations which usually occur within the wall. You would still be able to accurately call offside from this position.

Throw-Ins

It is most important that the touch line out-of-bounds call is not made until the ball has gone *completely* over the line either in the air or on the ground. It is equally important that you be in the proper position when making this call. No one should be able to question your call if you are standing on the line at the time the ball goes out of bounds.

When the ball goes out of bounds at or close to a 90° angle, it is rather simple for the player handling the throw-in to determine the spot where he should make the toss. However, when the ball crosses the line while nearly paralleling it, the situation becomes more difficult for the player and, most often, he will move too far downfield before taking the throw. Consequently, you end up having to blow your whistle to bring him back to the proper spot or have him throw it again if you did not catch him in time. Both situations are unnecessary and embarrassing to you and to the player and could easily be prevented by pointing to the spot where the throw-in should be taken before or as the player is given the ball by the ball person. (Fig. 34)

It is most important, however, that you make this signal after you have lowered your signal indicating the team's direction, because, by displaying them simultaneously, you may confuse many people across the field who will not know what each signal means. By pointing in one direction indicating the team to throw it in and pointing to the spot with the other hand, they will not know whose throw it is.

Your attitude toward the throw-in must be to allow the player to get the ball back into play as fairly and as quickly as possible. Do not be picayune over where the ball is thrown in. However, never allow a player to gain an advantage by throwing the ball in at a spot other than where it went out. While this may, many times, take the form of moving too far downfield, it may also mean moving backward far enough to allow him to throw it to his own goalkeeper.

In making sure that the throw-in is executed properly, you should stand on the touch line, but not too close to the player making the throw. Standing on the line places you in the best position to see if and when the ball enters the field of play. Of course, if it does not enter the field, the throw should be retaken. This position will also enable you to discern the placement of the player's feet during the throw.

Standing too close to the player taking the toss should be avoided,

Figure 34. **Indicating the Throw-in Spot. This signal is given after you have lowered your directional signal and only if you think that the player needs help in locating the spot.**

because, in doing so, you will concentrate on the player's arm motion and not be able to see that his feet are planted properly or vice versa. By standing at least ten yards away, it will help you get a better view of the entire throwing action.

When detecting an illegal throw-in, you should blow your whistle and then imitate the faulty action. This could entail the lifting of one foot to indicate that both feet were not on the ground at the time of the throw. You might also raise one hand over your head while using a throwing motion with the other hand to show that both hands were not used equally. Once the infraction has been demonstrated, you should point in the opposite direction for the other team to take the throw. Again, if there is enough time to do so, you should also briefly explain to the player what he did wrong and what he should have done.

When watching the throw-in, the near official (to the player taking the throw-in) usually has a good *side* view of the throwing motion. Consequently, he can best see how the feet are used and whether or not the ball is brought back behind the head. However, the near official is not in a good vantage point to confirm that both hands are used equally. Conversely, it sometimes happens that these observation angles are reversed.

This is why the far official should always be alert and ready to make the call for a throw-in violation if the near official does not. In making this call, however, the far official should wait a second or two to enable the near official to make the call. This will help make the near official look better because he will be making the decision. If he does not make the call, you have no choice but to assume that he has not seen the infraction and you should blow your whistle and make the call yourself.

This should not be interpreted as one official stepping on his partner's toes. To the contrary, it should be readily recognized that when an official is watching a player's actions, regardless of whether it is a throw-in or just regular play on the field, he can only concentrate on one area of the player's body at one time. This is merely one of the many instances in which the teamwork of the officials must materialize.

Handling the Ball

How you view the "hands" call could make you or break you more than any other call that you would make during a game. Consistency is of paramount importance here, and not only by being consistent yourself, but also by being consistent with your partner's philosophy on this call.

A good way to look at handling-the-ball is to ask yourself, "Did the player's hand or arm move in order to touch the ball?" Or, "Did the ball ricochet off of his body, another player or the ground and touch his hand or arm when it was in a normal position"? (Having one's hands or arms above one's head or shoulders should not be considered a normal position.)

If your answer to the first question is "Yes", then your whistle should be sounded and the direct free kick awarded. If it was unintentional, as described in the second question, then in accordance with NCAA rules, you must raise your clenched fist quickly and shout "Play On". (Technically, you should give the unofficial "no-call" signal as was discussed in Chapter Four and illustrated in Figure 15; however, the play-on signal, in this case, would be more emphatic and convincing.)

It is most important that you do not award a direct free kick for an accidental handling of the ball, because if you make that type of a call in the middle of the field, you will force yourself to make the same call in the penalty area in order to remain consistent. Naturally, in doing so, you are virtually giving goals away through the penalty kicks which you would be awarding to the other team.

Another type of handling-the-ball infraction, which unfortunately has become prevalent in recent years, is when the player, who sees himself beaten by his opponents, manages to deliberately grab the ball or slap it down in order to prevent his opponents' offensive attack. (Fig. 35) Not only should a direct free kick be awarded, but a yellow card, for unsportsmanlike conduct, should go with it. This type of play should not be considered as good defense, but as being harmful to the success and enjoyment of the game. Your yellow card will, once again, set the tone for the remainder of the game.

Perhaps this should be a point which you would want to discuss with the captains in your pre-game briefing. If, after having done so, this type of infraction occurs, you can rightfully look to the player's team captain for help in making sure that his team would not be guilty of that type of play again. Generally speaking, the extent to which players abuse the game in this manner is in direct proportion to how strict you are in making the call initially.

Goal Kick

When the offense causes the ball to go over the end line and it distinctly crosses the line to the right or left of the goal, the defensive players usually have no difficulty placing the ball within the proper half of the goal area for the ensuing goal kick. However, when a shot-on-goal flies over the crossbar, the defensemen will usually take a guess by placing the ball on one side or the other. They may also ask you, as the lead official at the time of the shot, for directions. If you allow them to guess as to where to place the ball, you will, more than likely, have to correct them. (And, of course, no one enjoys being corrected all of the time.) If they have to ask you for help, then, in essence, they are pleading with you to do your job. The proper procedure, in this case, should be for you to blow your whistle, point up field with your

Figure 35. Deliberately Handling the Ball. This violation is definitely not within the spirit of the game and must be dealt with immediately.

left hand while announcing, "Put it on the far side", or "Place it over here". This adds to your control of the game because you have given the players the answer to their question before they even thought of asking it.

When many defensive players place the ball for the goal kick, they will take every advantage that you will allow them to take. This is usually in the form of spotting the ball a foot or two outside of the goal area. NCAA rules state that the ball must be *within* the goal area, while FIFA rules allow it to rest on the line. In either case, it should not be allowed to be kicked from outside the area.

If you enforce this on your first goal kick of each period, then you will have *set the tone* for the goal kicks at your end of the field for the remainder of the period. Naturally, it is most important that your partner is as equally insistent on this matter as you are. Furthermore, remember that it would be very difficult to enforce this rule late in the game if you have been loose on it up until that point, especially if a coach notices it (late in the game) and complains about it.

Many players grow up with the game thinking that the ball *must* be placed on the *corner* of the two goal area lines. (Fig. 36) This has usually evolved from spotting the ball as far away from the goal mouth as possible as a protective measure. When the player tries to set it up directly on the corner, he

Figure 36. **The Myth of Where to Place the Ball for a Goal Kick. It does not have to be spotted on the corner of the goal area, but merely within that half of the goal area nearest to where it crossed the goal line.**

usually has difficulty keeping it from rolling because of the many layers of field lining material which have accumulated there or because of the depression in the ground which exists due to erosion. In both cases, the game is delayed while everyone stands by anxiously waiting for him to steady the ball. You could prevent this by telling the player to place the ball onto the grass just inside the line. Not only would he be more strictly in compliance with the rule, but the kick would be taken with less delay of the game.

On the goal kick, the best place for you, as the near or trail official, to stand is even with the corner of the penalty area (i.e. the 18-yard line) and between it and the touch line. (Fig. 37) In this manner, you will be able to ensure that the ball completely clears the penalty area untouched. You will also be in position to make sure that all opponents of the kicking team are out of the penalty area before the kick is taken and remain outside until the ball has cleared the area. Furthermore, this position will enable you to easily get back to cover any shot-on-goal in the event that the goal kick is immediately returned by the other team.

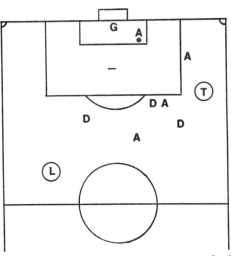

Figure 37. Positioning of Officials on a Goal Kick.

Above all, remember that the ball is not in play until it completely clears the penalty area untouched after having been kicked by the player taking the goal kick. Here is a true-life example of how this rule can be misinterpreted: In a youth game, an eight-year-old fullback scuffed the ground while taking the goal kick, consequently moving the ball only a few feet from its spot in the goal area. Being frustrated and embarrassed and unaware of the rule, he quickly moved forward and kicked it again.

The near official, who was the younger of the pair, blew his whistle and called for the goal kick to be retaken because it had not cleared the penalty area. However, his partner rushed in to declare that because the fullback had played the ball twice in succession, it should be an indirect free kick for the other team at the spot where the ball was played for the second time.

The two officials then got together to discuss it. Because everyone was watching and the junior official saw that his partner was not going to give in to his reasoning, he no longer pressed the issue and administered the indirect kick. After returning home, the junior referee called his commissioner for the interpretation and found that he had been correct in calling for the retake of the goal kick. He also vowed to never again allow himself to get overruled by a partner who is incorrect.

Corner Kick

To many players and observers, the corner kick is one of the more exciting and dramatic plays evolving from a dead-ball situation. Of course, this stems from the fact that, given a decent kick into the goal mouth, a score is quite possible. Consequently, this brings to bear great pressure on both officials in that they must be on top of the play with their eyes beamed both high and low to ensure that everyone involved plays the ball fairly. This is very difficult, because there may be as many as 20 players in on the action in front of the goal.

This is the reason that *both* officials must be close by on a corner kick. Many times, there is a tendency on the part of the trail official to hang back near the half-way line in anticipation of a fast break in his direction from an errant corner kick. There is the other trail official who feels that the corner kick is his partner's problem and not his. There is no excuse for either type of thinking. An official should be in good physical condition and have no difficulty dropping back quickly from a corner kick if the need arises.

When the corner kick is taken at the lead official's near corner, he should position himself just out of bounds (in case the ball hits him and so that he does not block the players' view) and at the junction of the goal area line and the goal line. (Fig. 38) He should make sure that the ball is placed properly within the quarter circle and that the corner flag post is not disturbed in any manner. He should give the direct-kick signal (and blow his whistle in those games where the second whistle is expected) as soon as the ball has been placed properly and is stationary. While some will feel that a signal is unnecessary for a corner kick, it does not hurt to give it as a reminder to the goalkeeper that a goal may be scored directly from a corner kick.

As soon as the kick is taken, the lead official should watch that the ball does not go completely over the goal line in the air. This becomes most evident when the ball flies directly over the official's head. Once he has determined that the ball will remain in play, he must turn quickly, move onto the goal line and focus on the players around the spot where the ball will land.

While all of this has been going on, the trail official has moved to a position near the outside corner of the penalty area. (Fig. 38) Since he knows that his partner will be concentrating initially on the kicker, the trail official must give his undivided attention to the movements of the players jockeying for position in the goal mouth. Obstruction of the goalkeeper is a common violation committed here. If these players are seen nudging and leaning on

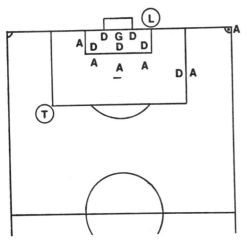

Figure 38. **Positioning of Officials on a Right-Front Corner Kick.**

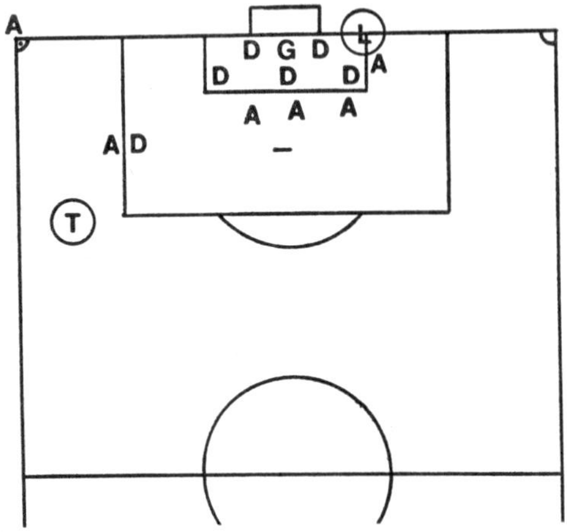

Figure 39. **Positioning of Officials on a Left-Right Corner Kick.**

each other to a substantial degree prior to the kick, it would be wise for the trail official to announce, "All right, be careful now—no holding and no obstructing". Since these players have been looking toward the kicker's corner, they have probably not noticed the trail official's movement into the area. Furthermore, they would see that the lead official is concentrating on the kicker and so it would be natural for them to think that their ploys are going unobserved. This announcement would alert them to "minding their manners" as the kick is taken.

When the kick is taken in the coffin corner, the trail official should move down as far as the 18-yard line but only five to ten yards into the field in case the kick is sent up field instead of into the goal mouth. (Fig. 39) The trail official is now responsible that the ball is placed properly but it is still the lead official who must signal for the direct kick (and blow his whistle, if necessary).

The trail official would also make certain that no defenders are within ten yards of the ball at the time of the kick. Once the ball has been kicked, the trail official must direct his attention to the players in the landing area.

The lead official, meanwhile, has moved onto the goal line at the junction of the goal area line, to view of the action. (Fig. 39) Being on the line allows the lead official to watch for out-of-bounds as well as for a score. Obviously, his chances of being hit by the ball are rather slim in this situation. Furthermore, since everyone's attention is focused away from the lead official, it would be good preventive officiating on his part if he were to let it be known, prior to the kick, that everyone should, "Be careful".

Penalty Kick

One of the most critical calls which an official can make during a game is that which results in a penalty kick. In practically every case, a goal is scored from a penalty kick. What this means is that you can have no doubt in your mind when you blow the whistle for a direct-kick offense which occurs in the penalty area.

This is where the official, who insists upon keeping his whistle in his mouth, will get into trouble. Invariably, he will see a player unintentionally handle the ball and, on pure reaction, blow his whistle. This is where another official will be described as "inconsistent" because during the early part of the game he has been making pushing and charging calls on incidental contact, but then he fails to make these calls for the same type of contact when it occurs in the penalty area. Violations which are committed intentionally should be called no matter where they occur and violations which are committed unintentionally should not be called no matter where they occur.

Since the call for a penalty kick is so crucial to each team, once you have blown your whistle to make the call, proceed in a decisive manner. First of all, make sure that your whistle is loud enough and sharp enough to stop play. The time-out signal should be given and the clock stopped. Secondly, make your violation signal distinctly while announcing the violation simultaneously *and* identifying the violator authoritatively. Then move directly and crisply toward the penalty-kick line and point, with a direct-kick signal, while announcing, "Penalty kick".

If you show indecision on any call which you make, you will lose respect. If you show indecision in making a penalty-kick call, you could lose control of the entire game. Everyone must be convinced that you saw the violation and called it without hesitation. Pointing out the number of the player committing the foul will lend support to your call. In fact, in doing so, his teammates will usually get more upset at him for causing the penalty kick than mad at you for calling it. Once you have made the call, carry on immediately with your responsibilities in setting up the kick.

In most cases, the lead official will make the call which results in a penalty kick usually because he is closer to the play than is his partner. Of course, that is not always the case as many trail officials have made this call. However, whenever a trail official makes this call, he must be certain that his position and view of the infraction cannot be questioned. Once again, presence lends conviction.

No matter which official makes the call for a penalty kick, each has certain duties which he should perform immediately. The trail official should move quickly into the penalty area and instruct all of the players, other than the goalkeeper and the player designated to take the kick, to leave the penalty area, to include the arc.

Once all of the players have taken their places, he should get their attention and then announce, "Remember now, do not cross that line until the ball has actually been kicked, and let's not have any talking during the kick". This type of preventive officiating should prevent any retakes of the kick, which usually cause more problems and ill-feelings toward the official than anything else.

The trail official should then take a position at the corner of the penalty area so that he will have a good view of any movement along the line. (Fig. 40) He should also keep an eye on the kicker to make certain that he kicks the ball properly.

Meanwhile, the lead official should retrieve the ball and briskly pace off twelve yards from the midpoint of the goal line and draw a two-foot line in the turf with his shoe. If the penalty kick mark (line) has not been obliterated through normal play and he had confirmed, during his pre-game field inspection, that it had been accurately measured and marked, he could dispense with his own pace-off.

Once he has determined the location of the penalty kick mark, he should place the ball on the center of it. The kicker may move the ball anywhere along that line if he so desires. After placing the ball, the lead official should ask, "Who is going to take the kick?" Once the player has acknowledged that he will be the one, the official should warn him by saying, "Remember

Figure 40. **Positioning of the Trail Official on a Penalty Kick.**

not to kick the ball until I have blown my whistle". This is another example of preventive officiating.

The lead official should then walk up to the goalkeeper and remind him of his responsibilities during the kick. The official should say, "Now, remember that you must have both feet on the goal line and you may not move them until the ball is actually kicked. If you move either of them too soon and he misses the shot, then I'll have to give him another one". Naturally, this type of preventive officiating should not sound like a threat, but more like a friendly reminder for the goalkeeper.

The official should then move to his spot to get the best view of the play. While doing so, however, he should look over his shoulder to make sure that the kicker is not moving to play the ball prematurely. The official should stand just inside the goal line and about four to five yards away from the near goal post. (Fig. 41) This distance is not too close to the play nor too far removed from it and affords the best vantage point for determining a score.

Since the trail official is watching for any infringements by the kicker, the lead official should place his hands on his knees, to show his readiness to make the call, and then blow his whistle sharply. Knowing that he must be alert to the possible illegal early movement of the goalkeeper's feet, the official should keep his eyes on the goalkeeper and his ears trained on listening for the sound of the ball being kicked. This method is essential as it is rather difficult to watch the ball being kicked and the movements of the goalkeeper at the same time.

With regard to substitutions being made before the penalty kick is taken, none may be made by either team from their bench areas. However, any defensive player on the field may replace the goalkeeper simply by notifying the official. Naturally, the players should exchange shirts. Furthermore, if a penalty kick must be retaken, the goalkeeper and/or the kicker may be replaced but, once again, only from the players already on the field.

If a penalty kick is being taken after the expiration of any period, it would be wise for you to move all of the players away (at least 20 yards) from the penalty area while explaining to them that, in this case, only the kicker may play the ball and he may play it only once. This will prevent any member of the kicker's team from playing the ball in the event it deflects off of the goalkeeper or the goal post and back into the playing field. The kicker should also be reminded that, he too, will not be allowed to play the ball again in the event of a rebound.

Insofar as time keeping during a penalty kick is concerned, NCAA rules require that the clock be stopped as soon as the official gives the time out signal. The clock should be restarted as soon as the ball is put into play, i.e. it has been kicked in a forward direction at least the length of its own circumference. If a goal is scored, the clock, technically, should start as soon

Figure 41. Positioning of the Lead Official on a Penalty Kick.

as the ball is put into play and stopped again as soon as the ball crosses the line. Since this is normally just a fraction of a second, it is common practice not to restart the clock unless the shot is missed.

Offside

Once the game has begun, you must determine how the team in your half of the field sets up its defense. This is most important so that you will be prepared to be in the proper position to make the offside call. When the ball is in your partner's half of the field and you are the trail official, you should be frequently looking over your shoulder, especially when the ball is dead, to see how the defensive players in your half of the field are playing. More than likely, the goalkeeper will be staying fairly close to his goal area. However, the player with whom you must concern yourself is his next closest teammate or that second defensive player who will determine the imaginary line by which your offside call will be governed.

Is that second defensive player also remaining close to his goal and/or penalty area or is he playing up around the center circle? He may even be in the offensive half of the field. You must be aware of where he is at all times, because as soon as the other team gets the ball, they will be attacking in your direction and, many times, that first kick is to the player streaking on a fast break. Of course, where that streaking player is compared to where the second defensive player is *at the time the ball is played* is the determining factor for your offside call (as long as the offensive player is in his opponent's half of the field).

If you are in the proper position to make the call, no one should object. However, if you are out of position and unable to make the call when many players, coaches and spectators can see the offside materialize better than you, you have virtually given the offensive team an undeserved goal while digging yourself a grave with regard to gaining or regaining game control or player respect for the rest of the game.

Other defensive stratagems for which you must be alert are the offside trap and the quick clear-out. The offside trap is sometimes used while the ball is in play, but, most often, it is employed on a free kick when a goal is imminent.

As an example, the attacking team has been awarded a direct free kick about thirty yards out from the goal. The defensive players will usually make their four-or-five-player wall about twelve yards from the ball and, as part of their strategy, all other members of the defensive team will not be any closer to their goal line than the wall itself. As expected, the attacking team will place several players just in front of the wall (between the wall and the ball) or to the side of the wall ready to break toward the goal as soon as the ball is kicked. (Fig. 42)

Figure 42. Players Preparing for the Offside Trap. Prior to the kick, the players in the light jerseys are onside, but...

Figure 43. Players Completing the Offside Trap....just before the ball is played, the dark-jerseyed players move up causing the light-jerseyed players to be offside—a legal play.

The offside trap is executed by having each member of the defensive team's wall move about two yards toward the kicker just before he makes contact with the ball. Since the attacking players are concentrating on the ball being kicked and, at the same time, leaning toward the goal, they usually are not aware of the defensive team's maneuvers and find themselves guilty of being offside at the time of the kick. The offside trap is a very smart defensive move and quite legal. (Fig. 43)

The quick clear-out usually occurs when a team's goalkeeper saves a shot and kicks the ball up field as fast as he can. At the same time, all of his defensive teammates quickly move up field ready to go onto the attack. If they maintain possession of the ball directly from the goalkeeper, they may have their opponents outmanned on a fast break. On the other hand, if the opponents intercept the goalkeeper's kick and try to counterattack quickly themselves, they will, usually, pass the ball to one of their forwards who will find himself offside because only the goalkeeper will be between him and the goal line.

To prevent the offside, of course, the forwards must retreat with the defensive players clearing out in order to get back onside. You, as the lead official, will find that you will be in for a running afternoon, because you will always be forced to clear out along with that second defensive player in order to be in position to make that next offside call.

When officiating a game in which one team is very confident that their defensive players are quick enough to get back on defense in the event of a fast break by their opponents, you may find the fullbacks playing up near mid-field or even in the offensive half of the field when their forwards are on the attack. In this case, you will find the forwards of the other team, standing near the half-way line, but just inside their half of the field, as they know that they cannot be offside in their own half of the field. (Fig. 44)

As the official who would have to make the offside call in the event the ball were to quickly change hands, you must be aware of these players and their location in relation to the half-way line. And remember, it is where the offensive player is at the time the ball is played that determines offside.

As soon as a team goes onto the attack, you must be watching for anyone being offside. When you see a player in an offside position, and he is seeking to gain an advantage, be ready to blow your whistle. As soon as the ball is played, make the call. The best way to determine whether or not to penalize a player for being in an offside position is to ask yourself, "Is he participating in the play?" If not, then do not call it offside.

A delayed whistle at this point could be very detrimental to you in the minds of everyone else. The delayed whistle is hardly ever interpreted as the time you needed to confirm that the player was actually offside. Invariably, everyone will think that you do not understand the rule and are making the

Figure 44. Watching for Offside Near the Half-Way Line.

call based upon where the player is when he receives the ball as opposed to where he is at the time the ball is played.

In making the offside signal, be sure to place both hands on your hips. Immediately thereafter, point to the player offside and announce his number. The proper signal will inform everyone as to what you have called and pointing out the player will assist the defense in quickly locating the spot where they are to put the ball back into play.

Some officials simply blow their whistles and point to the player offside. If the players are accustomed to looking at the proper signal (hands on hips), they will become confused at this half-signal. If a call is worth making, then everyone deserves to see the proper signal.

Improper signaling of offside quite often results in a series of errors on the part of the official which makes both of them look bad. It usually happens when the ball goes over the end line immediately after the lead official has blown his whistle for a player being offside. The official makes an improper or unclear signal or no signal at all and both of the coaches interpret it to mean that a goal kick has been called. They immediately notify the nearby trail official that they want to make some substitutions. The trail official, also interpreting the signal as a goal kick, beckons the players onto the field and turns to blow a series of short blasts on his whistle to indicate to his partner to hold up play while the player changes are being made.

Not realizing the confusion that his poor offside signal has caused, the lead official gets upset that his partner is allowing substitutions to be made at the "improper" time and pounces on his whistle, exclaiming, "No, no. No substitutions on offside". Meanwhile, about eight to ten players and substitutes stop dead in their tracks and wonder what is going on.

By the time all of the players return to their original positions on the field and the substitutes go back to their respective benches, many of them thinking that the officials have kept them from getting their chance to play, you and your partner have lost considerable ground in trying to show everyone how well you work as a team—and all because of a careless signal.

Drop Ball

When there are unusual delays or injuries during play, you usually want to restart the game as quickly as possible. The drop ball restart should be rather simple to execute, but, quite often, the game is delayed even more because one or both of the players involved kick the ball before it touches the ground.

While you might be quick to blame the players for not letting the ball hit the ground, you ought to reevaluate your technique instead. Two faults normally found here are dropping the ball from a height too high and telegraphing the initial downward movement of the ball.

As a preventive measure, you should remind both positioned players to "Wait until the ball has touched the ground before playing it." Secondly, hold the ball no higher than thigh level and drop or push it to the turf as quickly as possible, making certain, however, that both players are ready. Furthermore, since an official being hit by the ball, once it is played from a drop, is not uncommon, it is still another reason for not carrying your whistle in your mouth.

Use of Yellow and Red Cards

The procedure of issuing or displaying yellow and red cards for the appropriate infractions must be considered one of the most effective rule changes ever made in the game. Furthermore, it will not be at all surprising to see similar card systems incorporated in sports such as football, basketball, baseball, wrestling and tennis. They have recently been adopted for volleyball tournaments.

As a soccer referee, you must not be reluctant to issue a card when it is appropriate to do so. If a player or coach deserves to be issued a yellow or red card, issue it. If you hesitate or if you choose to ignore an obvious display of one of the yellow- or red-card offenses, you will do your fellow officials a disservice by nurturing inconsistency within your officials association.

Never think that unsportsmanlike conduct and dissent with the official will subside just because you let it go early in the game. In essence, you have, once again, set the tone for the game and you will find that it will be very difficult to make such calls later on when you have chosen to ignore them initially.

Always handle your yellow-card delivery with firmness, but in a constructive manner so that the player or coach will be able to recognize his wrongdoing with the thought that it will not happen again. Using sarcasm or harsh-sounding threats at this time will simply serve to antagonize and alienate the players toward you for the remainder of the game.

On the other hand, when you decide that you are going to issue a card, you must be quick to react to the offense, decisive in your actions and concise with your call. Making a big demonstration or going through a long lecture with the player will merely defeat the purpose of the card system and, once again, make him, his coach, his teammates and his followers more hostile toward you than you deserve.

In being quick to react to the offense, as well as being decisive in your actions, it is most important that you know exactly where your cards are and can get to them quickly and easily. There would be nothing more unimpressive for you to be fumbling in your pockets or socks looking for the proper card. While you would not want to be considered the "Fastest Card in the West", the principle of gaining respect through positive and decisive actions (such as that given the "Fastest Gun in the West") would be the same.

If your shorts have two pockets, you could always keep the yellow card in the right one and the red card in the left one. This would apply to double-pocketed shirts also. Some officials slip the yellow card inside the top of their right sock with the red card in their left sock.

If you prefer to carry them in your pockets, but you have only one pocket in your shorts or your shirt, you could make certain that the yellow card is always in front of the red one or cut ¾" off your red card so that you will always be able to grasp the proper one immediately. No matter what system you use, it helps if you do not have to look at the card itself before displaying it to the offender.

When you have decided to issue a yellow card, blow your whistle sharply, signal for the clock to be stopped, stop your watch and beckon the player to come over to you by saying, "Number 13, red, come here please". As he starts to approach you, you should walk to meet him. Do not stand there rigidly as if you were calling your dog or as if it were beneath your dignity to meet him halfway. When you and the player are within six feet of each other, stop and raise the yellow card at arms length over *your* head (not his).

This is so that no one will have any doubt as to what you are doing. You should never stick the card immediately in front of the player's face nor wave it at him in an aggressive manner. In the case of unsportsmanlike conduct, you should make the appropriate signal by placing the palm of your other hand onto the back of your head.

At the time you are giving the signal, you should be explaining to the offender exactly why you are issuing him a yellow card. It is most important that you use the proper words. In the cases of "entering and leaving the field without permission", "dissent with the official" and "persistent infringement of the rules", infractions for which there are no particular signals, it is imperative that you *accurately* announce or explain them to the player and his coach. You must be careful in your choice of words. For example, you cannot say that you are issuing a yellow card, "because he pushed the other guy too hard". That is not a yellow-card offense and a coach could lodge a valid protest on you for issuing a yellow card for that reason. This actually happened. If, indeed, the push was too hard, you should issue the yellow card for "unsportsmanlike conduct" or issue the red card and eject him for "violent conduct".

Not only should the offender and his coach know why you have issued a card, your partner must be informed also. The reason for this is simple. If you have issued a yellow card to "blue number 16" for "dissent" in the first half without notifying your partner, he could issue the same player a yellow card later in the game and not realize that he should have given him a red card for his second cautionable offense. Needless to say, it would prove to be most embarrassing when the opposing coach would protest the discrepancy and the official would be forced to take out his red card for the player once the coach was found to be correct. It would help your partner and the scorer if you were to maneuver the carded player around so that both of these individuals could easily read his number.

Having good communication between officials is most important when it involves the issuing of cards, but it is also helpful to take an extra moment to write down the offender's number and team in the event that any other cards are issued during the game. It is rather difficult to remember all of them and, of course, you never know how many you and your partner are going to have to issue.

When a player is issued a yellow card, the official closer to the carded player's coach should ask the coach if he would like to make a substitution for his player. If he chooses to make a change, it is only appropriate that the same official would ask the opposing coach if he would like to make a similar number of substitutions. These substitutions are allowed under NCAA rules.

In issuing a red card and ejecting a player, once again, it is vital that this be done with authority. If the infraction is obvious and occurs in full view of everyone, especially the offender's coach, you merely need to pull out your red card, hold it over your head and with your other hand point to the offender and then point to the team's bench, indicating where he is to go upon his ejection. Current NCAA rules also require that the ejected player leave the premises of the field—to the team bus or locker room. If neither are available, he is permitted to remain with the spectators.

If the infraction, such as "using foul or abusive language" occurs away from the coaches view or hearing, you should go through the same motions of ejecting him, but then go as far across the field as you need to go in order to inform his coach of your call. By going toward the coach, you are using the initiative to keep him abreast of the situation, while, at the same time, preventing him from getting all upset by not knowing what is going on and yelling out to you, "Hey, ref. What was that for?"

In dealing with coaches and issuing cards to them for their conduct, it is most important that you, once again, use the art of preventive officiating. If coaches are guilty of any infringement of the rules, it is usually "dissent with the official". Dissent by the coach seems to surface in two categories. In one instance, the coach will grunt and groan ever so slightly in the early stages of the game to express displeasure over some of yours or your partner's judgment calls. These groans, such as "Aw, c'mon ref", will usually increase in intensity later on if allowed to.

The second instance involves the coach who has behaved impeccably during the game, but then chooses to protest a judgment call by blurting out, at the top of his lungs, something like, "What? You gotta be kidding. What kind of a call was that?"

In dealing with the first coach, you should make sure that he is not permitted to continue with his verbal abuse. Nipping it in the bud is most important, because, as was indicated earlier, his attitude will begin to be reflected in his players' behavior. That short, sincere statement from you to him made privately may be all that is necessary to impress upon him your feeling about his conduct. If you were to say something like, "C'mon, coach, please direct your comments toward your team and then I will be able to better concentrate on calling a good game", in a sense, you will have placed some of the burden of officiating the game onto his shoulders.

Needless to say, in reacting to the second coach, or a coach in the first instance who does not comply with your advice, you have no choice but to issue him a yellow card for "dissent". While you may not want to embarrass the coach in this manner, most coaches will react by saying to themselves, "Well, I guess I can't mouth off with these officials". Furthermore, while most would not admit it, they will respect you more for taking such a stand.

When Your Partner Fails to Show Up

For one reason or another, and usually once each season, you will be faced with working a game alone because your partner does not show up. Naturally, you should get to the nearest phone immediately and call him or your commissioner with the hopes of getting him to the game or at least ascertaining that he is on his way.

When all efforts fail, you should inform both coaches. If the coaches will permit you to work the game by yourself, then you should oblige them. (Some leagues will not allow a game to be played with just one official.) Naturally, the coaches will be sympathetic with your problem at hand, but do not expect them to be pleased with the situation. After all, it is your fellow official who has let everyone down and given a "black eye" to your officials association.

Your only recourse is to work the diagonal or the longitudinal axis of the field in the same manner as the single referee works with two linespersons under international mechanics. The only difference, of course, is that you will not have experienced linespersons helping you with offside and out-of-bounds calls as well as with other infractions.

You should seek help from each of the coaches for knowledgeable assistant coaches and spectators who could serve as linespersons. If you are convinced that they understand the offside rule then you could have them wave a shirt or bright cloth whenever they detect such an infraction. If they do not understand the offside rule, then you have no choice but to make that call yourself. In this case, you should warn both teams that if a player looks close to being offside, then you will, more often than not, blow your whistle for the infraction unless you are able to get into position to more accurately make the call.

In order to cover balls going over the touch line, you should have the linesperson raise his hand whenever the ball goes completely over the line. You should still reserve the right to determine which team will take the throw-in unless your view was blocked and you seek help from that linesperson.

The same philosophy should apply to goal line calls, however, you should do everything in your power to be in good position to make all shot-on-goal calls. Working the game by yourself is hard work, but you cannot feel sorry for yourself. In fact, you owe it to the players, coaches and spectators to call the game as well as you and your partner would have.

CHAPTER VI

After The Game

Once the timer's horn or your final whistle has indicated the end of the game, your only concern should be to leave the field. You should, however, meet your partner halfway, shake hands and walk off the field together with the same degree of dignity that you displayed when you entered it.

If at all possible you should avoid walking near the losing coach and team. While they may not pin the blame for their loss on you, they just might want to do exactly that if you give them the opportunity by passing near their post-game huddle.

By the same token, do not hang around the field waiting for compliments, as you just might find yourself in the middle of a group representing or following the losing team. Furthermore, no matter what you would say to these people, you would never get a chance to defend any of your calls. The best way to avoid this kind of post-game treatment is to do exactly that—avoid it. Simply do not allow yourself to get into such a predicament in the first place.

If you like to receive compliments on your officiating, and most referees do, you should understand that the best compliment you can receive is *silence*. When no says anything—good or bad—to you after the game, it usually means that you have been as inconspicuous as possible and that both teams have considered the results of the game to be an indication that one team simply outplayed the other in a controlled atmosphere and in accordance with the rules.

The ultimate compliment is the good feeling that you have inside of you as you walk off the field that you have done the best job that you could have possibly put forth. Therefore, if you want to derive anything from officiating each game, it should be the two S's—silence and self-satisfaction. (Or is that three S's?!)

84

CHAPTER VII

Rules

AUTHOR'S NOTE: As in most games, the players involved in a sandlot game or the league's rules makers have the right to play the game of soccer under whatever rules they care to adopt. They may choose to abide by the rules of a recognized national or international governing body or they may want to play the game using a combination of rules from each of the rulebooks. They may even elect to incorporate rules of their own in order to better meet their needs and objectives. The following represents a description of the basic rules of soccer as played in most areas of the country. Known rule variations are noted where appropriate.

I. **FIELD REQUIREMENTS**
    A. THE FIELD OF PLAY should be rectangular with the recommended maximum lengths and widths as follows:

Age of Players	Length	Width
Over 17	120 yds. (110m)	75 yds. (68.6m)
14-17	110 yds. (100m)	65 yds. (59.5m)
Under 14	100 yds. (91.5m)	55 yds. (50.3m)

   B. The FIELD should be marked with highly visible, straight (or properly curved, where appropriate) lines. The longer boundary lines are called TOUCH LINES (sometimes side lines), while the shorter boundary lines are called GOAL LINES (sometimes end lines). These lines should meet at the corners; that is, the goal lines should extend across the field of play, including between the goal posts, and the touch lines should extend the entire length of the field of play. In no manner should the lines be constructed so that they would endanger the players.
   C. The HALF WAY LINE should be marked across the field of play equidistant from the goal lines. The center of the field should be designated by an appropriate mark and a circle with a ten-yard (9.15m) radius drawn around it.
   D. At each end of the field of play two lines should be drawn at right angles to the goal line, 18 yards (16.5m) from each goal post. These should extend into the field of play for a distance of 18 yards (16.5m) and be joined by a line drawn parallel with the goal line. Each of the spaces enclosed by these lines and the goal line is called a PENALTY AREA.
       At each end of the field, a two-foot (0.61m) line should be placed at a distance of 12 yards (11.0) from the midpoint of, and parallel to, the goal line. This line

SOCCER FIELD

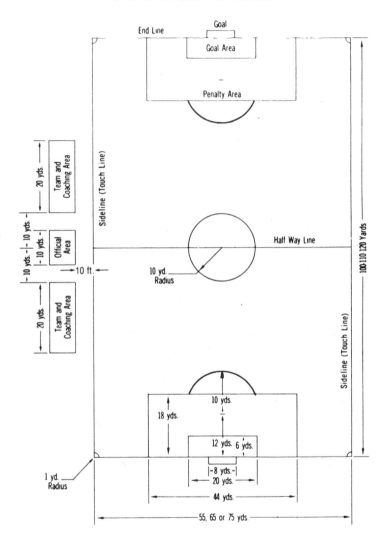

End Line

Goal

Goal Area

Penalty Area

20 yds.

Team and Coaching Area

Sideline (Touch Line)

10 yds. — 10 yds.

10 yds.

Official Area

10 ft.

Half Way Line

10 yd. Radius

100-110-120 Yards

20 yds.

Team and Coaching Area

Sideline (Touch Line)

10 yds.

18 yds.

12 yds. 6 yds.

1 yd. Radius

|-8 yds.-|
20 yds.

44 yds.

55, 65 or 75 yds.

should extend one foot (0.30m) on either side of the undrawn center line. The penalty kick may be taken from any position on this line.

Using the center of this penalty kick line, a 10-yard (9.15m) arc should be drawn outside the penalty area and closing on the penalty area line. This serves as a restraining line during penalty kicks.

E. At each end of the field of play two lines should be drawn at right angles to the goal line, six yards (5.5m) from each goal post. These should extend into the field of play for a distance of six yards (5.5m) and be joined by a line drawn parallel with the goal line. Each of the spaces enclosed by these lines and the goal line is called a GOAL AREA.

F. From each corner, a quarter circle, having a radius of one yard (1.0m), should be drawn inside the field of play. Each of the quarter circles is called a CORNER AREA.

G. The HOME TEAM must always make certain that the field of play meets the requirements of the two teams or the league. In the event that the field remains playable but on which, during the game, the lines and markings become invisible due to snow etc., the lines and markings are to be assumed to exist and the officials' decisions should be made accordingly.

II. GAME EQUIPMENT

A. The GOALS should be placed at the midpoint of each goal line and consist of two wooden or metal posts, equidistant from the corner flags and eight yards (7.32m) apart (inside measurement), joined by a horizontal crossbar of similar material, the lower edge of which should be eight feet (2.44m) from the ground. The width and depth of the goal posts and the width and depth of the crossbar should not be less than four inches (10.16cm) nor more than five inches (12.7cm) and should be painted white.

B. The GOAL NETS should be attached to the uprights, crossbar and ground behind each goal. They should be firmly pegged down to the ground and put in order before every match, and care taken that there are no openings for the escape of the ball. The nets should be properly supported so that the top of the net will extend backward on a level with the crossbar for a distance of about two feet (0.61m) from the crossbar to allow the goalkeeper ample room.

C. A CORNER FLAG, consisting of a flag on a post not less than five feet (1.5m) high, should be placed at each corner. A similar flagpost may be placed opposite the halfway line on each side of the field of play, not less than one yard (1.0m) outside the touch line.

The corner flag should be not less than five feet (1.5m) high from the surface of the ground. The post should have a rounded top and should be at least 1½ inches (3.81cm) thick. The corner flag may not be removed for any purpose during the game. The flag itself should be of a bright color, easily distinguishable from the surroundings, and should be about two feet (0.61m) long by one foot (0.30m) wide and securely fastened to the post.

D. The TEAM BENCHES and the TIMER'S TABLE should be placed on the same side of the field and a minimum of ten feet (3.05m), if possible, from the touch line. Furthermore, it is recommended that some form of restraining line be erected to keep spectators at least ten feet (3.05m) from the touch line.

E. The BALL should be spherical with the outer casing made of leather. No material should be used in its construction which might prove dangerous to the players. All balls used in a game should be of the same make, and furnished by the home team. The ball should not be more than 28 inches (71.12cm) nor less than 27 inches (65.58cm) in circumference. The weight of the ball at the start of the game should not be more than 16 ounces (454.4g) nor less than 14 ounces (397.6g), and the weight should not exceed 16.75 ounces (475g) even when wet and used.

III. THE PLAYERS, THEIR UNIFORMS AND EQUIPMENT

A. The NUMBER OF PLAYERS permitted to start a game on the field for each team is not more than eleven, with one serving as the goalkeeper. (VARIATION: Some leagues allow a lesser number, such as seven or eight, to start in order to minimize the chances of a forfeited game.) Any number of players may participate in a game, including overtime periods and tie-breaking procedures. They may be substituted or resubstituted without limitations. (VARIATION: Some leagues permit only a certain number, eighteen for example, to participate in a game.) It is recommended that an agreement between the teams' representatives be reached concerning the number of substitutes well ahead of a scheduled game.

B. A PLAYER'S UNIFORM should consist of a jersey or shirt, shorts, stockings and soccer-type shoes. Shin guards are strongly recommended for safety purposes. (Some leagues may require them to be worn.)

C. PLAYERS ON THE HOME TEAM should wear white or light-colored shirts, while the visitors should wear dark-colored shirts. Goalkeepers should wear colors which distinguish them from all others on the field, to include the opposing goalkeeper and the officials. (Teams should also refrain from wearing all-black uniforms if the officials from their local association usually wear the all-black uniform.)

D. NUMERALS, at least six inches (15.24cm) in height, must be worn on the back of each player's shirt, while numerals at least four inches (10.16cm) in height must be worn on the front of each player's uniform.

E. SHOES must meet the following specifications: Cleats or studs are to be at least ½ inch (1.27cm) in diameter and not project more than ½ inch (1.27cm) (VARIATION: ¾ inch (1.27cm) from the sole or heel of the shoe. Aluminum, leather, rubber, nylon, or plastic cleats with steel tips are legal if they conform to the width and length requirements. (VARIATION: Metal or metal-tipped cleats are illegal.) It is strongly recommended that all players be equipped with and wear legal, molded-sole soccer shoes.

F. ILLEGAL EQUIPMENT is not to be worn by any players. If, in the referee's opinion, an article of equipment is considered dangerous or confusing, it must be removed before the player may start or continue to play. The use of any hard or dangerous protective equipment, including casts, is prohibited even though covered with soft padding. (VARIATION: In some leagues, these items may be used if covered to the satisfaction of the officials.) A player wearing any equipment not in compliance should be sent off the field temporarily. He should not return without first reporting to the referee, who is to satisfy himself that the player's equipment is in order. Then the player may re-enter the game, but only at a moment when the ball is not in play.

IV. MAKING SUBSTITUTIONS

A. SUBSTITUTIONS ARE ALLOWED by either team under the following conditions:
1. On a goal kick. (VARIATIONS: Substitutions are allowed only for the team taking the goal kick. Substitutions are allowed by their opponents only if the team taking the goal kick makes a substitution.)
2. On a corner kick. (VARIATIONS: Similar to the conditions described above for a goal kick.)
3. After a goal has been scored.
4. Between periods.

5. In the event of an injury. Only the player(s) injured may be replaced. If the injured player(s) is(are) replaced, their opponents may substitute a like number. (VARIATION: Opponents may not substitute.)

6. When a player is cautioned (yellow card). Only the player(s) cautioned may be replaced. If the cautioned player(s) is(are) replaced, their opponents may subsitute a like number. (VARIATIONS: Neither team may substitute when a yellow card is displayed. If a player is disqualified, he may not be replaced; however, both teams may make any number of substitutions at that time.)

7. (VARIATION: A team having been awarded a throw-in may make any number of substitutions. Their opponents, however, may not.)

(PENALTY — Indirect free kick against the offending team from the location of the ball at the time the illegal substitution is discovered.)

B. In REPORTING INTO THE GAME, a substitute must first report to the official scorer, remain at the scorer's table and be recognized by the referee when he enters the field. (VARIATION: In the absence of an official scorer, the coach should notify the nearest referee of his intent to make a substitution.) No player who has left the field of play with or without the permission of the referee after a game has started may return to the field or participate in play without first reporting to the referee.

Any player who leaves the field during the progress of the game, except through normal movement of play, without the permission of the referee is guilty of unsportsmanlike conduct.

(PENALTY — Indirect free kick from the location of the ball at the time of the infraction.)

To facilitate the making of substitutions, it is required that a noise-producing instrument of quite different tone from the timekeeper's signaling device be used. A horn is suggested.

C. In CHANGING GOALKEEPERS, from either the bench or by a player on the field, the referee must be notified. The new goalkeeper must also be wearing an acceptable shirt.

(PENALTY — Failure to notify the referee will result in an indirect free kick if the ball is handled within the penalty area by the non-reporting goalkeeper.)

V. **SYSTEMS OF OFFICIATING AND BALL HOLDERS**

A. A REFEREE WORKING WITHOUT APPROVED LINESPERSONS, is responsible for making all calls in the game. He must make every attempt to be in position to make all calls. It is recommended that he select two linespersons from those attending the game to assist him making out-of-bounds calls. Each linesperson should have a flag or something to wave when the ball goes completely over the touch or goal line. However, the referee would remain responsible for determining which team would put the ball back into play.

B. A REFEREE, WORKING WITH APPROVED LINESPERSONS, is responsible for the game. A linesperson may indicate, by waving his flag, that he has detected a violation, such as tripping or dangerous play. The referee, however, has the option of recognizing or ignoring his linesperson's flag. Regarding offside and out-of-bounds calls, however, the referee usually honors his linesperson's judgment since his view of these plays is normally much better than that of the referee's.

C. In the DUAL-REFEREE SYSTEM, both officials shall have equal authority and responsibility in the calling of fouls and violations on any part of the field at any time.

D. AT LEAST TWO BALL HOLDERS, in each of the officiating systems mentioned

Rules

above, should be provided by the home team. Their primary duties are to carry an extra approved game ball and serve as ball retrievers in order to allow only minimal delays in the game. The ball holders are not expected to make any calls. Nevertheless, their performance is under the direct supervision of the officials.

VI. **THE OFFICIALS, THEIR UNIFORMS, JURISDICTION AND DISCRETIONARY POWER**

A. The accepted UNIFORM should be either a black and white, vertically striped shirt or a black shirt with white collar and cuffs, worn with black shorts, black stockings with white tops and black footwear. (VARIATIONS: Some associations permit all-black or all-white caps, black jackets, black gloves and black warm-up pants to be worn in adverse weather conditions. Shirts may have long or short sleeves.) When more than one approved referee is working a game, all must be dressed alike.

B. A REFEREE'S JURISDICTION begins from the time he enters the field of play, and his power of penalizing extends to offenses committed when play has been temporarily suspended or when the ball is out of play. *He should, however, refrain from penalizing in cases where he is satisfied that by doing so he would be giving an advantage to the offending team. When the referee observes a foul which he is not to penalize, he should call out the words "play on" and raise his hand (fist closed) over his head to indicate that he has seen the foul.*

The referee must signal on all fouls. He must also notify the timekeeper for all time outs, and confirm for the scorekeeper the players to be credited with goals and assists. (VARIATION: These are optional responsibilities.)

The referee shall allow no person other than players and ball holders to enter the field of play without his permission. Trainers and coaches may enter the field only if called by the referee.

C. The referee has the DISCRETIONARY POWER to stop a game for any infringement of the rules and to suspend or terminate the game whenever, by reason of the weather, condition of the field, interference by spectators, or other cause, he deems such stoppage necessary.

The referee may caution any player or coach of misconduct or unsportsmanlike behavior (persistent infringement of any of the rules of the game) and, if he persists, suspend him from further participation in the game. When cautioning a player or coach, the official shall display a yellow card and indicate the individual concerned. The second card displayed to the same individual is to be a red card. When suspending a player or coach, a red card is to be displayed. A suspended player must leave the premises of the field of play. (VARIATIONS: A suspended player need not leave the premises. Coaches cannot be cautioned.)

The referee may forfeit a game to the opposing team if, in his judgment, a coach prolongs a discussion with the referee or refuses to leave the field at the request that he do so.

The referee may stop a game if, in his opinion, a player has been seriously injured. If, in the referee's opinion, the player is slightly injured, the game should not be stopped until the ball has ceased to be in play. A player who is able to go to touch line or goal line for attention of any kind should not be treated on the field of play.

VII. **TIMING AND SCORING THE GAME**

A. There shall be one OFFICIAL TIMER designated by the home team. It is recommended that a knowledgeable individual perform this function. Before the game the referee should instruct the timer as to his duties. He should arrange

Rules

with the timer an understandable series of signals, covering time outs, substitutions, termination of playing periods and out of bounds.

The timer should use one stop clock or watch that is visible at all times. An extra clock and signaling device should be available for immediate use if necessary.

The timer's responsibilities include:

1. Keeping track of playing time and stopping the clock when signaled by the referee to do so; when a goal is scored; when a penalty kick is awarded; and when a player is carded.
2. Start the clock when the ball is put into play; and signaling the referee when a substitution is to be made.
3. Keeping track of the half-time interval and notifying the referees and teams two minutes in advance of the start of the second half.
4. Calling off audibly to the nearest official the last ten seconds of playing time in any period, and signaling for the the termination of the period.
5. Signaling with a gun or horn (not whistle) when time has expired.
   NOTE—The expiration of time is the moment when the timer's signal starts, regardless of the position of the ball.

B. The LENGTH OF THE GAME should be two equal periods, unless otherwise mutually agreed upon. In the case of a tie two extra periods should be played. The score of the game should then stand as official, with the following exception: Time should be extended beyond the expiration of any period only to permit a penalty kick to be taken.

The recommended maximum time periods are as follows:

Age of Players	Minutes/Half	Minutes/Overtime Period
Over 17	45	10
14-17	40	5
Under 14	35	5

(VARIATIONS: The total time for the game is divided into four equal quarters. Tied games remained tied with no over-time periods played. Tied games are determined by sudden-death overtime periods, i.e. first team to score wins the game. Tied games are determined by a penalty-kick competition, or some similar contest of skills.)

C. The HALF-TIME INTERVAL should not exceed ten minutes except by consent of the referee and both coaches.

D. PERIODS MAY BE SHORTENED by the league or, if mutually agreed upon, or in any emergency by agreement of the coaches or by order of the referee, provided it is done before the game or before the second half begins so that all remaining periods are the same length.

E. A GOAL IS SCORED when the entire ball passes completely over the goal line, between the goal posts and under the crossbar. Being on the line is not over the line. The ball may roll along the goal line and even be partly over the line and yet not be called a goal. The goalkeeper may even be behind the line and play the ball in front of the goal, thus preventing a goal. It is the position of the ball which counts, so that it is not impossible for the goalkeeper to be on his own goal line or in front of his goal line with the ball in his possession and because he carries the ball over the goal line, he scores a goal against his team.

A goal can only be scored when the ball is not thrown, that is, impelled by the hands or arms of a player, other than the goalkeeper, of the attacking side, or carried by the hands or arms of the attacking player.

F. Should the CROSSBAR BECOME DISPLACED for any reason during the game, and the ball is across the goal line at a point which, in the opinion of the referee, was below where the crossbar should have been, he should award a goal.

G. A GOAL COUNTS ONE POINT. The team scoring the greater number of goals during a game is the winner. If no goals, or an equal number of goals are scored, the game is recorded as a "Tie". The score of a forfeited game is recorded at 1-0.

VIII. **STARTING AND RESTARTING PLAY AND WHEN TO BLOW THE WHISTLE**

A. A COIN TOSS shall be used by the referee to allow the captain winning the toss to choose either to kickoff or to defend a goal in the first period.

B. The KICKOFF may be taken only after the referee has blown his whistle. The game is actually started when the player makes this place kick (i.e., a kick at the ball while it is stationary on the ground in the center of the field of play) at least 27 inches (69cm) into his opponents' half of the field of play. Every player is to be in his half of the field and every player of the team opposing that of the kicker is to remain at least 10 yards (9.15m) from the ball until it is kicked off. A goal may not be scored directly from the kickoff. A kickoff is an indirect free kick. The kicker may not touch the ball a second time until it has been touched by another player. (PENALTY—Indirect free kick from point of infraction.)

C. IF THE BALL IS NOT KICKED OFF INTO THE OPPONENT'S HALF OF THE FIELD, the ball must again be placed on the kickoff mark and properly kicked forward. After the ball has been properly kicked off it may be kicked in any direction. Any player who repeatedly kicks off improperly, willfully encroaches on the 10-yard (9.15m) distance or willfully moves beyond his own halfway line should be cautioned, and on repetition, ordered off the field.

D. AFTER A GOAL IS SCORED, the ball is to be taken to the center of the field and kicked off under precisely the same conditions as when the game was started, by the team against which the goal was scored.

E. TEAMS ARE TO CHANGE ENDS of the field at the start of the second half, and play should then start with a kickoff by a member of the team opposite to that of the team taking the kickoff at the start of the game. If overtime is necessary, teams shall change ends to start each overtime period, with the teams continuing to alternate kicking off to start subsequent periods.

F. THE BALL IS OUT OF PLAY when it has completely crossed a boundary line, whether on the ground or in the air. Even if the ball has landed within the field after being beyond the line in mid-air, it is still out of bounds. It is also out of play when the game has been stopped by the referee. The referee must blow his whistle when the ball is out of play. (VARIATION: The referee may blow his whistle when the ball is out of play.)

G. THE BALL IS IN PLAY at all other times from the start of the match to the finish, including rebounds from a goal post, crossbar or corner flagpost into the field of play. If the ball rebounds from either referee when he is in the field of play, it is still in play.

H. A BALL IS PUT BACK INTO PLAY, after having been out of play, in the following ways:
   1. When the ball crosses a touch line, a throw-in is used to put it back into play.
   2. When the ball crosses a goal line, either a goal kick or corner kick is used to put it back into play.
   3. When the game has been temporarily suspended for an injury, deflated ball etc., except when a free kick or throw-in has been called for, the referee

should drop the ball at the spot where it was when play was suspended. The ball is considered to be back into play when it touches the ground. If the ball is played before it touches the ground, the ball is to be dropped again. If play was stopped with the ball in the penalty area, the ball is dropped at the nearest spot outside the penalty area. (VARIATIONS: The ball is dropped at the appropriate spot regardless of whether or not it is in the penalty area. If a team is in clear possession of the ball when play is stopped, they are awarded an indirect free kick to restart play from the spot where the ball was when play was stopped.)

4. When a goal is scored, a kickoff is taken by the team scored upon. (Refer to VIII. B.C.D.)

I. THE REFEREE MUST (VARIATION: MAY) BLOW HIS WHISTLE to indicate that:
   1. The ball has gone out of bounds;
   2. A foul, rule infraction or violation has occurred;
   3. Play is to be stopped for an injured player;
   4. A period has ended;
   5. A goal has been scored;
   6. A kick off may be taken;
   7. A penalty kick may be taken;
   8. A free kick may be taken (but only after telling the kicker and the other players to wait for his whistle);
   9. Play may be restarted after a substitution has been completed;
   10. Play may be restarted after play had been stopped for an injury, a player or coach being carded or an unusual delay.

IX. **OFFSIDE**

A. A PLAYER IS OFFSIDE if he is nearer his opponents' goal line than the ball is at the instant the ball is passed toward him unless:
   1. He is in his own half of the field of play;
   2. There are two of his opponents *nearer* to their own goal line than he is;
   3. The ball last touched an opponent or was last played by him;
   4. He receives the ball directly from a goal kick, a corner kick, a throw-in, or when it is dropped by the referee.
   (PENALTY—Indirect free kick from point of infraction.)
   NOTE: The fact that a player is in an offside position does not cause the referee to call the violation immediately. The player must be gaining an advantage or seeking to do so by being in the offside position. (PENALTY—Indirect free kick from point of infraction.)

B. A PLAYER CANNOT BE OFFSIDE:
   1. If he is not ahead of the ball when it is last played;
   2. If he is ahead of the ball when it is last played by one of his own side, he must have two opponents between him and the opposing goal line;
   3. If he receives the ball from an opponent;
   4. When an opponent last plays the ball;
   5. On a corner kick, goal kick, drop ball or throw-in.

C. ONCE OFFSIDE, A PLAYER CANNOT PUT HIMSELF ONSIDE UNLESS:
   1. An opponent next plays the ball;
   2. He is behind the ball when it is next played by one of his own side;
   3. He has two opponents between him and their goal line when the ball is played by one of his own side farther from the opponents' goal line than himself.

NOTE: The ball rebounding off a goal post or the crossbar does not put a player onside who was offside when the ball was last played.

X. FOULS, VIOLATIONS AND MISCONDUCT

A. A player should be penalized if he is guilty of INTENTIONALLY KICKING, STRIKING, ATTEMPTING TO KICK OR STRIKE, KNEEING, TRIPPING OR JUMPING AT AN OPPONENT.

1. Tripping includes throwing or attempting to throw an opponent by the use of the legs, or by stooping in front of or behind an opponent in such a manner as to cause him to fall or lose his balance.

2. Jumping at the opponent is not jumping into the air to play a ball, which is jumping upward. Deliberate tripping, kicking, striking, or jumping at an opponent or attempting to do so is dangerous and liable to cause injury. The referee should caution the player who attempts it, advising that a repetition of the action will necessitate the player's being ordered off the field. The referee may order the player from the field on the first offense if the action is flagrant. A player so disqualified may not be replaced.

3. A sliding tackle is a legal tackle when one or both feet are used in an attempt to tackle the ball which is in the possession or control of an opponent and it is made within the normal peripheral vision of the opponent and the initial contact is with the ball.
(PENALTY—Direct free kick from point of infraction.)

B. A player should be penalized for INTENTIONALLY HANDLING, CARRYING, STRIKING OR PROPELLING the ball with a hand or arm. This does not apply to goalkeepers in their own penalty area.
(PENALTY—Direct free kick from point of infraction.)
NOTE: UNINTENTIONAL HANDLING occurs when the ball strikes or touches the hands or arms of a player. This should not be penalized even though the advantage gained by the unintentional handling may go to the offending team or player. (VARIATIONS: Moving the hands or arms to protect oneself should be considered intentional handling; however, girls are permitted to protect the chest area provided their hands and arms remain in contact with the body. Boys are permitted to protect the groin area in the same manner.)

C. A player should be penalized if he HOLDS OR PUSHES an opponent with his hand or hands, or with his arm extended from his body. Holding includes the obstruction of a player by the hand or any part of the arm extended from the body. Under no circumstances is a player permitted to push an opponent with his hands or arms.
(PENALTY—Direct free kick from point of infraction.)

D. A player should be penalized if he CHARGES AN OPPONENT VIOLENTLY OR DANGEROUSLY. A fair charge consists of contact with the near shoulder, when both players are in an upright position, within playing distance of the ball, and have at least one foot on the ground and their arms held close to the body.
(PENALTY—Direct free kick from point of infraction.)

E. A player should be penalized if he INTENTIONALLY PLACES A HAND ON AN OPPONENT in order to get to the ball.
(PENALTY—Direct free kick from point of infraction.)

F. A player should be penalized for CHARGING INTO AN OPPONENT WHO IS IN THE AIR in an attempt to receive or play the ball.
(PENALTY—Direct free kick from point of infraction.)

G. A player who INTENTIONALLY CHARGES THE GOALKEEPER when the

94

goalkeeper has possession of the ball, should be disqualified (red card) from the game without warning.

(PENALTY—Direct free kick from point of infraction.)

H. A player should be penalized if he KICKS OR ATTEMPTS TO KICK THE BALL when it is in the GOALKEEPER'S POSSESSION.

(PENALTY—Indirect free kick from point of infraction.)

I. A player should be penalized if he OBSTRUCTS AN OPPONENT when not playing the ball, that is, runs between an opponent and the ball or interposes his body as to form an obstacle to an opponent.

(PENALTY—Indirect free kick from point of infraction.)

J. A player should be penalized for engaging in DANGEROUS PLAY. Examples include:

1. Raising the foot in an attempt to play the ball to the level of and close to an opponent's shoulder or head when the opponent is in a normal stance;
2. Hitch-kicking or double-kicking within six feet (1.83m) of an opponent;
3. Lowering the head to a level of the waist or below in an attempt to head the ball in the presence of an oncoming player;
4. Withholding the ball from play by covering it while it is on the ground;
5. Projecting the foot forcefully downward toward an opponent's lower legs in an attempt tackle the ball. This is known as the "plunger kick."

(PENALTY—Indirect free kick from point of infraction.)

NOTE: Usually when dangerous or potentially dangerous play is observed by the referee, he will caution the offender against a repetition. But dangerous play may likely be of such a character as to warrant the referee's sending the offender off the field without a caution.

K. THE GOALKEEPER HAS CERTAIN PRIVILEGES, within his own penalty area, which are not given to any other player. He may carry, strike or propel the ball with his hands or arms. Furthermore, he may not be charged, interfered with or impeded in any manner by an opponent while he is in possession of the ball. Possession includes the act of dribbling the ball with the hand and also the dropping of the ball for the kick. Outside the penalty area, the goalkeeper has the same privileges as any other player.

L. The GOALKEEPER should be penalized if he VIOLATES HIS PRIVILEGES.

1. When in possession of the ball, the goalkeeper may not carry the ball more than four steps while holding, bouncing or throwing the ball in the air and catching it again, without releasing it so that it is touched by another player. Furthermore, the goalkeeper must not deliberately delay getting rid of the ball when it is in his possession.

(PENALTY—Indirect free kick from point of infraction.)

2. The goalkeeper may not intentionally strike an opponent by throwing the ball vigorously at him, or push him with the ball while holding it.

(PENALTY (if offense occured in penalty area)—Penalty kick.)

M. In terms of MISCONDUCT, a player should be:

1. Cautioned (yellow carded) for:
   a. Persistently infringing upon any of the rules of the game, or acting in an unsportsmanlike manner.
   b. Objecting by word of mouth or action to decisions given by the referees.
2. Disqualified (red carded) for:
   a. Persisting in misconduct or for committing a second cautionable offense.
   b. Exhibiting violent conduct, i.e., using foul or abusive language, or in the

Rules

opinion of the referee, persistently infringing upon the rules of the game. (PENALTY: When play has been stopped by reason of a player being cautioned, ordered from the field or without a separate breach of the rule having been committed—the game should be resumed by an indirect free-kick to be taken by a player of the opposite team and from the place where the ball was at the time of the infringement.)

N. NON-PARTICIPANTS, that is, those other than the players and the ball holders, are not allowed on the field of play without permission from the referee. Trainers and coaches may enter the field only if called to do so by the referee.
(PENALTY—Indirect kick from location of ball at the time of infraction.)

O. COACHING FROM THE SIDE LINES is restricted to verbal commands, without the use of visual aids, with one's own team, and is confined to the immediate bench area. The referee should warn an offending coach that on a recurrence he will award an indirect free kick against his team given from the spot where the ball was when the violation occurred.

It is permissible for a player to call instructions to a player on his own team during the game, however, this should be penalized when it is done to intentionally distract an opponent.

XI. DIRECT FREE KICK OFFENSES

A. Handling the ball;
B. Holding an opponent;
C. Pushing an opponent;
D. Striking or attempting to strike an opponent;
E. Jumping at an opponent;
F. Kicking or attempting to kick an opponent;
G. Tripping or attempting to trip an opponent;
H. Kneeing an opponent;
I. Charging an opponent violently or dangerously;
J. Handling the ball by the goalkeeper outside his penalty area;
K. Illegally charging the goalkeeper in the penalty area;
L. Goalkeeper intentionally striking or attempting to strike an opponent by using the ball;
M. Charging from the rear unless being obstructed.
NOTE: All direct kicks awarded to the offensive team in the penalty area are to be taken as *penalty kicks* from the penalty kick line.

XII. INDIRECT FREE KICK OFFENSES

A. A player touching the ball a second time before it has been touched by another player at the kickoff, or a throw-in, or on a free kick, on a corner kick, or on a goal kick (if the ball has passed outside the penalty area);
B. A goalkeeper taking more than four steps while in possession of the ball;
C. A goalkeeper delays releasing the ball;
D. A substitution or resubstitution being made at an improper time;
E. A substitution or resubstitution being made without the referee being notified;
F. Persons other than the players and ball holders entering the field of play without the referee's permission;
G. Illegal coaching from the side lines after being warned by the referee;
H. Objecting by word or action to a referee's decision;
I. Unsportsmanlike conduct;
J. Dangerous play;
K. To resume play after a player has been cautioned or disqualified;

L. Offside;

M. Charging illegally (not violent or dangerous);

N. Interfering with the goalkeeper or impeding him in any manner until he releases the ball, or kicking or attempting to kick the ball when it is in his possession;

O. Obstruction other than holding;

P. Player leaving the field of play during the progress of the game except through normal movement of play without the consent of the referee.

XIII. **FREE KICKS**

A. A FREE KICK is taken to resume play after the play has been stopped by the referee for any of the offenses listed in Sections XI and XII. The kick is taken by a member of the team against which the offense is committed, and is taken from the spot where the infraction occurred.

Free kicks are classified as follows:

1. *Direct free kick* — A direct free kick is one on which a goal can be scored directly from the kick against the offending team;

2. *Indirect free kick* — An indirect free kick is one from which a goal cannot be scored unless the ball has been touched by a player other than the kicker before passing through the goal.

B. WHEN A FREE KICK IS BEING TAKEN, a player of the opposite team is not to be within 10 yards (9.15m) of the ball until it is in play, unless he is standing on his own goal line, between the goal posts. The kick should be retaken if a player is within 10 yards (9.15m) of the ball and intentionally interferes with the kick. If a player tries to delay the game by not getting 10 yards (9.15m) from the ball, he and the team captain should be cautioned, and if any member of the team repeats the same infraction, that player is to be removed from the game.

As soon as the ball is in position to be played, the referee must give a signal for the kick to be taken. This signal should be either the direct-kick or indirect-kick signal, whichever is appropriate. This signal may also be accompanied by the blowing of the referee's whistle. (VARIATIONS: The referee *must* blow his whistle for the kick to be taken as well as signal for the type of kick. The referee need not blow his whistle and he is required to signal for indirect kicks only.) The ball may be kicked in any direction. The ball must be stationary when the kick is taken, and is not in play until it has traveled the distance of its own circumference (27 inches, or 0.68m.) The kicker may not touch the ball a second time until it has been touched by another player.

(PENALTY — Indirect free kick from point of infraction.)

NOTE: When a free kick is awarded to the defending team in the penalty area, the ball must clear the penalty area. The goalkeeper may not receive the ball into his hands from a free kick in order to thereafter kick the ball into play, or the kick must be retaken. All opponents must be outside the penalty area and at least 10 yards (9.15m) from the ball, or the kick must be retaken.

XIV. **GOAL KICKS**

A. A GOAL KICK IS TAKEN by a member of the defending team when the ball passes completely over the goal line (excluding that portion between the goal posts and under the crossbar), either in the air on the ground, having last been played by a member of the *attacking* team.

B. The BALL IS PLACED on the ground at a spot within that half of the goal area nearest to where the ball crossed the goal line, and is kicked in any direction from that spot. The ball must clear the penalty area, or the kick is to be retaken. A goal may not be scored from a goal kick. The goal kick is an indirect free kick.

Players of the team opposing that of the player taking the goal kick are to remain outside the penalty area until the ball clears the penalty area line after the kick has been taken, or the kick is to be retaken.

The goalkeeper may not receive the ball into his hand from a goal kick in order that he could thereafter kick it into play. The goalkeeper may not pick up the ball and kick it. The ball must be placed on the ground and kicked from there.

The kicker may not touch the ball a second time after it has passed beyond the penalty area and before it has touched another player.

(PENALTY—Indirect free kick from point of infraction.)

XV.   CORNER KICKS

A. A CORNER KICK is taken by a member of the attacking team when the ball passes completely over the goal line (excluding that portion between the goal posts and under the crossbar), either in the air or on the ground, having last been played by a member of the *defending* team.

B. A MEMBER OF THE ATTACKING TEAM SHALL TAKE THE KICK from within the quarter circle at the nearest corner flag post, which must not be removed. A goal may be scored directly from a corner kick. A corner kick is a direct free kick.

Players of the team opposing that of the player taking a corner kick are not to be within 10 yards (9.15m) of the ball until the ball is in play, that is, has traveled the distance of its own circumference, or the kick is to be retaken.

The kicker may not touch the ball a second time after the ball is in play until it has been touched by another player. If the ball hits the goal post and rebounds toward him, he still may not touch the ball until it has been touched by another player.

(PENALTY—Indirect free kick from point of infraction.)

XVI.   PENALTY KICKS

A. A PENALTY KICK IS AWARDED for any infringement of the rules by the defending team within their penalty area which is penalized by a direct free kick. *The foul must be deliberate.* A penalty kick is to be awarded irrespective of the position of the ball, if the offense by the defending team is committed within the penalty area. A goal may be scored directly from a penalty kick. A penalty kick is a direct free kick.

A penalty kick must not be awarded for offenses which call for an indirect free kick, regardless of where or by whom the offense is committed.

B. The PENALTY KICK IS TO BE TAKEN FROM ANY SPOT ON THE PENALTY MARK LINE and when it is being taken, all players (except for the kicker and the opposing goalkeeper) are to be within the field of play, but outside the penalty area and at least 10 yards (9.15m) from the penalty mark.

The opposing goalkeeper must stand, without moving his feet, on his own goal line between the goal posts, until the ball is kicked. The player taking the kick must kick the ball forward the length of its own circumference in order for it to be in play. If the ball is not put into play properly, the kick is to be retaken.

The kicker may not touch the ball a second time until it has been touched by another player. If the ball hits the goal posts or the crossbar and rebounds into play, the kicker still may not touch the ball until it has been touched by another player.

C. If, during a penalty kick, there is an INFRINGEMENT:

1. By a member of the defending team, the kick is to be retaken if a goal has

not resulted; (The infringement is ignored if a goal is scored.)

2. By a member of the attacking team other than the player taking the kick, the kick is to be retaken if a goal has resulted; (The infringement is ignored and play is allowed to continue if no goal is scored.)

3. By the player taking the kick, a goal may not be scored and the kicker's opponents are awarded an indirect free kick from the spot of the infringement.

D. If the ball touches the goalkeeper before going into the goal when a penalty kick is being taken AT OR AFTER THE EXPIRATION OF TIME, it does not nullify a goal.

It necessary, time of play is to be extended at end of any period to allow a penalty kick to be taken. If a penalty kick is taken after the expiration of time, only the kicker may play the ball. If the ball caroms off the goalkeeper and goes directly into the goal, it should be counted as a goal.

XVII. THROW-INS

A. A THROW-IN IS TAKEN to put the ball back into play after it has passed *completely* over a touch line, either on the ground or in the air, from the spot where it crossed the line. It may be thrown in any direction by a player of the team opposite to that of the player who last touched the ball.

B. AT THE INSTANT HE RELEASES THE BALL, the thrower must face the field of play with part of each foot either on the touch line or the ground outside the touch line. The thrower is to use both hands equally and deliver the ball from behind and over his head. The ball is considered to be in play from the throw as soon as it crosses the vertical plane of the outside edge of the touch line. A goal may not be scored directly from a throw-in. A throw-in is regarded in the same manner as is an indirect free kick. If the ball is improperly thrown in, the throw-in is to be taken by a player of the opposing team.

The thrower may not touch the ball a second time before it has been touched by another player.

(PENALTY—Indirect free kick from point of infraction.)

XVIII.   RECOMMENDED REFEREES SIGNALS

XIX.   ADDRESS INFORMATION FOR OBTAINING OFFICIAL RULEBOOKS

For a copy of the Official Soccer Rules of the National Collegiate Athletic Association, write to the Editorial and Sales Offices, NCAA Publishing Department, P.O. Box 1906, Shawnee Mission, Kansas 66222 (913-384-3200). For a copy of the Soccer Rules of the National Federation, write to the National Federation of State High School Associations, Federation Place, Box 98, Elgin, Illinois 60120. For a copy of the FIFA Laws of the Game and Universal Guide for Referees, write to the Federation Internationale de Football Association, Hitzigweg II, Zurich, Switzerland 8032. For the USSF supplement to the FIFA Laws of the Game, write to the United States Soccer Federation, 350 Fifth Avenue, Suite 4010, New York, New York 10001.

OFFICIAL'S MANUALS

from Leisure Press

TOUCH AND FLAG FOOTBALL

John W. Reznik
And Rod Grambeau
University of Michigan

1979/88 pp./paper $2.25
ISBN 0-918438-46-2

> **OFFICIAL'S MANUALS**
>
> only **$1.35 each on 1-time purchase of 10 or more copies (any combination)**

BASKETBALL

Gary Miller
Cal State - Northridge

1979/72 pp./paper $2.25
ISNB 0-918438-47-0

VOLLEYBALL

James A. Peterson
And Lawrence S. Preo

1979/96 pp./paper $2.25
ISBN 0-918438-48-9

SOFTBALL

Robert Clickener
University of Illinois

1979/72 pp./paper $2.25
ISBN 0-918438-49-7

SOCCER

Nick Kovalakides
University of Maryland

1979/100 pp./paper $2.25
ISBN 0-918438-50-0

> • Use as a reference • Issue to your sports officials • A valuable aid for programs at *all* levels

Date P

O
S

**LEISURE
PRESS**

P.O. Box 3
West Point, N.Y. 10996
Tel (914) 446-7110

N

C